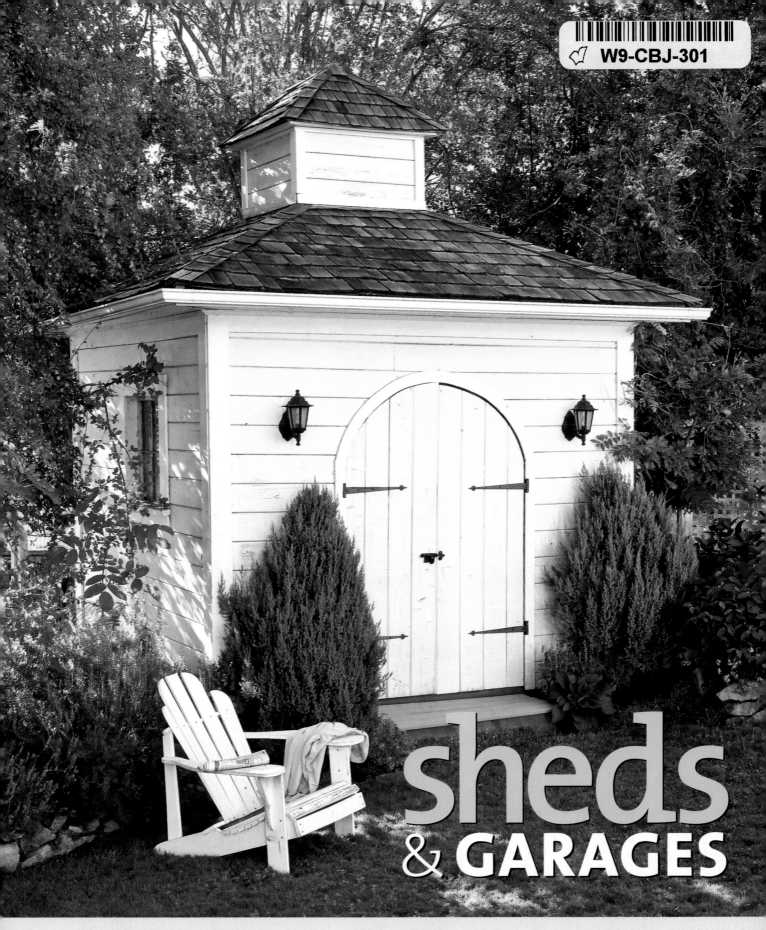

sheds
& GARAGES

by Scott Atkinson and the Editors of Sunset Books, Menlo Park, California

SUNSET BOOKS

VP, EDITORIAL DIRECTOR
Bob Doyle

DIRECTOR OF SALES
Brad Moses

DIRECTOR OF OPERATIONS
Rosann Sutherland

MARKETING MANAGER
Linda Barker

ART DIRECTOR
Vasken Guiragossian

STAFF FOR THIS BOOK

MANAGING EDITOR
Bonnie Monte

PAGE LAYOUT
Maureen Spuhler, Susan Paris

COPY EDITOR
Julie Harris

PRINCIPAL PHOTOGRAPHER
Jamie Hadley

PRINCIPAL PHOTO STYLIST
JoAnn Masaoka Van Atta

ILLUSTRATORS
Troy Doolittle, Bill Oetinger

PROOFREADER
Mary VanClay

INDEXER
Nanette Cardon

PREPRESS COORDINATOR
Danielle Johnson

PRODUCTION SPECIALISTS
Linda M. Bouchard,
Janie Farn

10 9 8 7 6 5 4 3 2 1
First Printing January 2008
Copyright © 2008, Sunset Publishing
Corporation, Menlo Park, CA 94025.
Third edition. All rights reserved,
including the right of reproduction in
whole or in part in any form.
ISBN-13: 978-0-376-01377-4
ISBN-10: 0-376-01377-X
Library of Congress Control Number:
2007932162
Printed in the United States of America.

FRONT COVER PHOTOGRAPHS
Main: Photo by Olson Photographic/Corner House
Stock Photo. Design by Better Barns.
Bottom (1): Photo by Jamie Hadley.
Design by Stuart Shepse. Builder: Lane Williams.
Bottom (2): Photo by Jamie Hadley.
Design by Chris E. Thomas and Barn Pros.
Bottom (3): Photo by Christopher Vendetta.
Design by Garlinghouse Company.
Bottom (4): Photo by Jamie Hadley.
Design by Michael Bond.

For additional copies of *Sheds & Garages* or any
other Sunset book, visit us at www.sunsetbooks.com.

For more exciting home and garden ideas, visit
myhomeîdeas.com

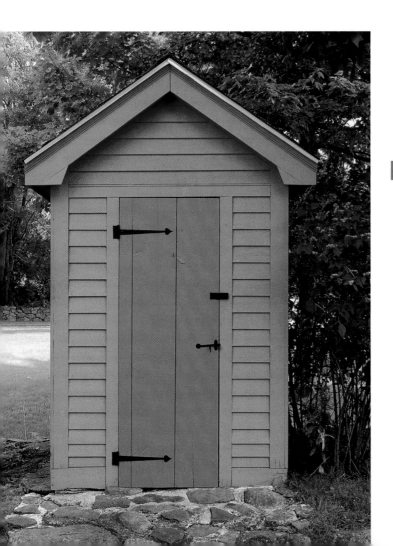

SIMPLE SPACES

WHILE IT MAY BE THE MOST FUNCTIONAL BUILD-ING ON YOUR PROPERTY, a shed, barn, or even a garage (the modern version of a barn) can have a distinctly romantic quality. Perhaps that's because it evokes a time of hands-on simplicity, when gardening and the care of animals were part of our daily rhythm. These no-frills structures carry echoes of a form-meets-function, rural lifestyle where pure usefulness had its own beauty.

And they're not just for tools and cars. Today's shed, garage, or barn can also be a destination in its own right with plantings, paving stones— even a decorative pond. With a few twists, your structure could be a greenhouse, an art studio, a home office, a playhouse, a teahouse, or a guest cottage. Larger structures may be divided up for several uses.

Perhaps best of all, an outbuilding makes an ideal project for a budding carpenter. Its basic nature is forgiving of less-than-perfect joinery and often requires little or no plumbing, wiring, or interior finish and trim. And it provides the chance to experiment with custom combinations of colors and materials.

Whether you're building, buying, or just browsing, this book has you covered—from the ground up. We kick things off with some plan-ning guidelines plus dozens of inspiring photos. Thinking of building it yourself? We survey the tools and materials you'll need. Next, take a tour of basic shed-building techniques—from founda-tions to finishing touches. Want specifics? You'll find plenty of step-by-step projects and "Designer's Sketchbook" ideas that you can build as is or adapt to your needs. Finally, we offer listings for kits and plans to buy and/or build.

So here's to finding that perfect blend of shelter, storage, style, and simplicity you've been yearning for. When your new space is ready, you might just find yourself spending more time there than in the house!

getting
started

WHAT ARE YOUR OPTIONS?

Great things can come in small packages. This shed may look tiny, but it still packs in plenty of pots and garden tools.

SOMEWHERE BETWEEN COZY LIVING SPACE and the great outdoors is a middle zone. This is where we store our garden tools, camping gear, and cars and bikes; where we pot plants, build boats, and pursue painting; and where we shelter farm animals and crops. Whether it's for storage, work space, or shelter, we turn to sheds, garages, and barns to provide protected space. The differences between these structures are largely ones of size and styling.

Sheds

A shed is a fundamentally simple structure. While the foundation may be as permanent as a concrete slab, it can also be as minimal as a pair of skids (page 62), if local codes allow it. Even a backyard deck can host a shed.

It's the details that make a shed special. Windows, doors, roof, siding, and interior trim can turn a leaky old outbuilding into a cozy, stylish retreat. Even a bland prefab or kit shed can dance new steps with a few custom touches.

RIGHT: Sheds make great getaways, like this tropics-inspired backyard bungalow smack in the middle of Northern California. The banana yellow paint and funky galvanized roof are reminiscent of an island beach hut. A small front porch forms a sheltered spot for watching the world go by.

LEFT: This prefab shed inspired by an old-fashioned barn is spacious enough for a painter's studio. Custom touches include the arched transom window and classic art-studio skylights. If your studio sits on top of a "temporary" foundation (page 62), you may not even need a building permit.

Garages

Think of a garage as a bigger, more formal version of a shed. A well-designed garage not only shelters cars and adds storage but also has distinctive architecture that either sets it apart from the house (see above) or matches it. Even a basic garage can mimic house details such as eave depth, siding and trim type, and window design.

Like a larger shed, the garage is likely to have a concrete slab or perimeter foundation. It also usually has electricity and may include plumbing for water and sewage. Sometimes there's a second-story living space or loft, plus interior amenities like built-in benches and cabinets.

This manufactured structure combines wide carriage doors with ramps for wheeling things in and out. Traditional touches include beveled siding, transom windows, and a cupola up top.

A former one-car garage is now a combination playhouse-storage space. A classic arbor and a scored concrete patio extend the living area.

ABOVE: **A big horse barn sports the classic overhanging eaves, sliding doors, and upstairs loft window. BELOW: This scaled-down, 18- by 24-foot working barn sits atop an easy-to-clean concrete slab and includes a separate wing for feeding and sheltering sheep. The upstairs door allows access to the storage loft above.**

Barns

Once basic shelter for animals and crops, barns are now larger, looser cousins of sheds and garages—multipurpose structures that house workshops, art studios, vehicles, and other equipment.

The charm of a barn is its no-muss, no-fuss aesthetic. It might have a bare earth floor or a more modern concrete slab. It usually has generously sized access doors. You can frame it like a house or shed (page 59) or use traditional pole or timber framing (page 61). Short on space? You can get the barn look on a shed footprint—and budget—by choosing a gambrel roofline (see page 25) and traditional barn styling.

ABOVE: Classic barn styling and spirit influenced the design of this working garden shed that's also a wonderful place to take a break. The sliding barn door allows easy access to garden equipment. The big window in back was salvaged from a construction project.

RIGHT: Big barns like this one are the ultimate in multitasking. Downstairs there's plenty of space for cars, trucks, snowblowers, or farm equipment. The upstairs loft has a photographer's office and studio. The trick to barn design is finding inspiration and scaling it down to fit your needs and footprint.

TAKING STOCK

YOU'VE SEEN SOME OPTIONS. Now it's time to start brainstorming. What, exactly, do you want your new structure to do, both now and in the future? Have you always wanted a place to make pottery? Or do you just need somewhere to stash the snowblower? You may find that a combination of work and storage space would be best for you.

Assessing Your Needs

For starters, grab a pen or your laptop and list every use you can think of for your structure. That's the easy part. The tougher part is paring the list to what's realistic.

Once you've narrowed down the function, the next step is to figure size. Of course, your site is a factor (pages 18–23), but when starting it's best to work from the inside out. If it's strictly storage you're after, make a list of everything you'll be putting inside your structure. What about the lawn furniture? The outdoor grill? Toys?

If you'll be working inside the structure, think about how much room you'll need to move around comfortably. What tools or furniture will be required? Also think about what utilities, if any, you will need. Hot and cold running water? Electricity? Heat? And don't forget about lighting. Although windows or skylights can provide natural light during the day, they won't be of much use in the evening.

No room for a standard shed? These custom-built storage units hang on an exterior house wall. Double doors swing open for easy access. A galvanized steel roof, made by a sheet-metal shop, covers each shed to channel off rainwater.

Blocking Out Space

A tape measure and a pad of graph paper are your best tools for laying out the interior space. Start by drawing an outline of your intended structure on graph paper—using a scale of ¼ inch per 1 foot works well. Then measure any large items you intend to store inside: car, bikes, boxes, workbenches, lawn mowers, etc.

Next, think about how all these items might be organized. Try to envision wall racks and bins for garden tools and sports equipment, shelving for potting supplies and small items. Pencil them inside your structure's outlines and check the recommended spacings on the facing page to make sure you've got plenty of room for movement.

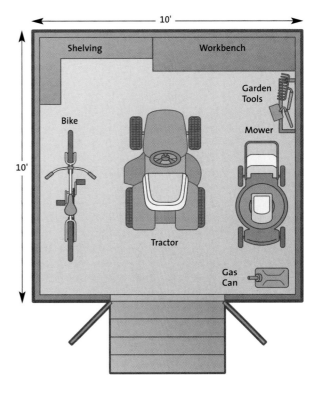

SHED SPACING

Allow at least a 12-inch zone around mowers, bikes, and boxes so you can walk around them with ease. Also, think about how you'll get at one piece of equipment without disturbing the others. This is particularly important if you're storing a riding lawn mower or other big item. One solution: Rather than centering the door, as shown at right, offset it to one side. Then store the biggest item against the side wall nearest the door, leaving the remaining space free for smaller supplies and equipment.

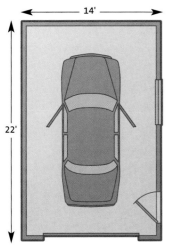

GARAGE SPACING

With today's wider vehicles, measuring is crucial to ensure you have adequate space for getting in and out comfortably, as well as for walking around inside the garage. Because most garages are also used for storage, make sure there's space for that, too. Also consider traffic patterns inside the garage to make sure there's convenient access to both cars and cabinets.

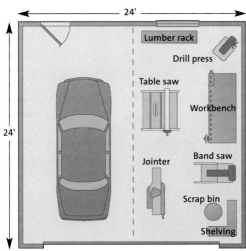

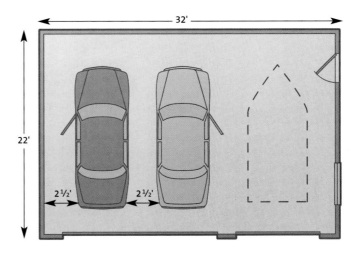

RIGHT: **Need more space? Look up! Here, the ground floor frames an open garage; living space occupies the upstairs. Easy-access barn doors slide on tracks mounted above the garage's openings.**

BELOW: **Think of it as a "family shed." The original plan included space for storing tools and potting plants— but it kept evolving. What the two adults and three kids, all with hectic schedules, really needed was a backyard retreat. By the time it was finished, it was more like a satellite family room, and it's now used for everything from desk work to summer dining. The new structure looks old, thanks to recycled wood and cozy furnishings.**

ABOVE: Outdoors it's cold and snowy, but inside this backyard office the weather's fine. The design makes efficient use of the tiny area by using built-ins —a wraparound work counter, bookshelves, and cubbyholes sized for computer components.

RIGHT: This handsome shed does double duty—thanks to its generous main space and a sheltered back alcove, which houses a potting bench and firewood. The whole structure, including the alcove, sits on top of a 10- by 12-foot concrete slab. For a look at the shed's front face, plus step-by-step building tips, see page 104.

THE RIGHT SITE

If you're planning a private retreat and you have the room, consider tucking your shed where you can get away from it all.

YOUR SHED'S LOCATION WILL HAVE A BIG IMPACT ON HOW USEFUL IT IS. Function offers some obvious clues: a potting shed should be near the garden, a private retreat tucked away, and an entertainment cabana near the main house or patio. Need water and electricity or phone and cable lines? You'll have to consider their accessibility. If you have a sloping site, you can flatten the grade and/or opt for a pier- or post-footing foundation (pages 62–63); stairs or ramps can provide access to a raised floor (pages 94–95).

Before you commit to a particular location and size for your structure, however, you'll need to consider building codes and zoning restrictions, sun exposure and seasonal conditions, and how the structure will look from your house or property line.

Code Concerns

In many areas, zoning restrictions and local building codes regulate where you can place your structure and how big it can be. To find out, consult with your building inspector. He or she will advise whether you'll need a building permit and inspection to make sure the structure meets the minimum code requirements.

In some areas, structures below a certain square footage—typically 100 to 120 square feet—are considered accessory buildings and don't require a permit. Also, sheds built on temporary foundations such as skids or piers, which can be moved, might not require a permit either. Permits may seem like a big nuisance, but they're in your best interest. An inspection can ensure that the structure you build will be sturdy and safe.

Be a Good Neighbor

Zoning restrictions are designed to prevent homeowners from encroaching on their neighbors. They're also aimed at creating a unified look, especially in historic sections and in neighborhoods with homeowners' associations.

The most commonly enforced restrictions govern lot coverage, setbacks, easements, and building height. Lot coverage limits how much of the property can be covered by buildings. A setback defines how close a structure can be built to another structure and to the property lines. An easement is an area that must be left accessible to people other than the homeowner (such as space near a power pole for utility worker access). Building height may be restricted as well. Apply for a variance if you believe your plans are within the spirit, if not the letter, of the law.

If your structure will house garden tools or supplies, take the shed to the garden. Here, a small clapboard-sided classic holds everyday needs close at hand.

How's Your Weather?

Once you've identified any restrictions, you can pick the final spot for your new structure. Think about access in all four seasons. What might seem an ideal spot in the summer might be inaccessible in the winter. Likewise, trees that provide privacy in the summer may leave your structure exposed in the fall. Beware of low spots; they'll drain poorly in wet weather.

For work spaces, consider the views you'll have out the windows and doorways of the structure. Also think about the quality of the light streaming in. South-facing openings admit lots of sunlight but also add heat and glare, while north-facing windows and skylights lend soft, even light.

Finally, walk around and observe how the structure will be viewed from your house or property line. If you're in doubt about the right site, stake out the perimeter of your proposed shed with mason's twine and stakes; study it at different times of day and, if possible, in different seasons.

OPPOSITE: Rather than lose planting space on her small urban lot, the owner of this backyard studio moved her garden onto the roof. Flowers and grasses grow in 5 inches of soil over a waterproof membrane, watered by drip irrigation. Floor-to-ceiling windows and a Dutch door are recycled construction materials; the shingles are sustainably harvested redwood.

BELOW: Sloping site? No problem. This prefab shed sits snugly behind a concrete retaining wall and atop a wood-post foundation hidden by lattice skirting. The windows, skylights, and sheltered front porch are custom additions.

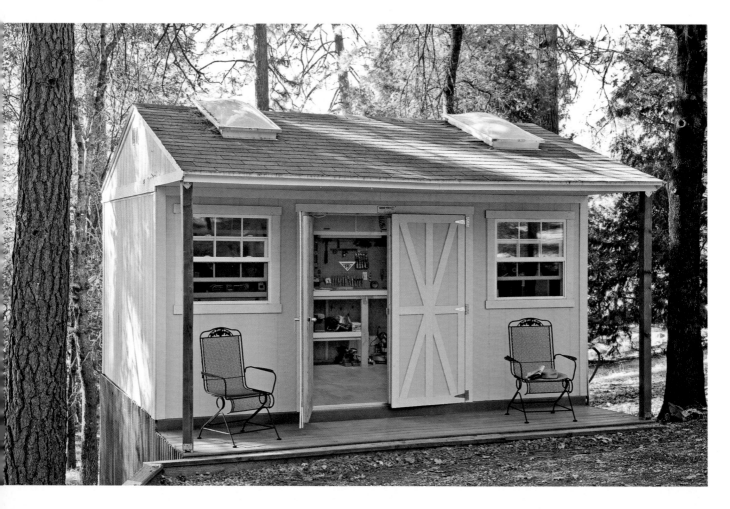

Potting sheds can serve as both garden headquarters and personal retreats. This weathered minibarn evokes the rural barn look without the barn's traditional size. Although it seems miles away from the busy world, it's only a short walk from the well-tended garden.

RIGHT: Orient a greenhouse for the amount of sun exposure you want. This one sits atop a perimeter foundation that accommodates the slope. It features shingled skirting below and polycarbonate greenhouse glazing above. Easy-care gravel and stepping-stones form the floor.

BELOW: Sometimes the best site is close at hand. Here, an added lean-to shares a wall with the garage woodshop.

WHAT'S YOUR STYLE?

ONCE YOU'VE PICKED YOUR STRUCTURE'S SIZE AND SITE, you can turn your attention to appearance. What profile looks best to you? Do you want to match a shed to your existing structures? Or are you after a totally different look?

Basic Shapes

The main profiles to chose from are lean-to, gable, saltbox, gambrel, and hip. There are also variations on each type. Though each style has a rectangular footprint, what sets them apart is the roofline, which is how the roof is framed and pitched.

Lean-to. A lean-to design has a single sloping roof (also called a shed roof). It's inexpensive and easy to frame, but headroom varies greatly from front to back.

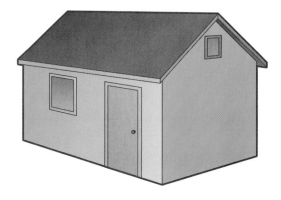

Gable. On a gable structure, the two halves of the roof join together in a classic triangular shape. Gable roofs are simple and economical to build and offer superior load-bearing and drainage capabilities.

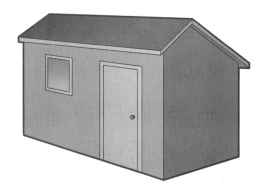

Saltbox. A saltbox is similar to a gable but the ridge is offset, providing more headroom at the front of the shed.

Details and more details help set the style. Have fun! This potting shed looks livelier than most, thanks to its scrolled trim, multipaned door and windows, and multicolor paint job.

Gambrel. A gambrel roof (named after the hindquarters of a horse) is basically a gable roof with two slopes or pitches on each side. Although more complex to frame, it offers significantly more headroom and storage space than a gable roof.

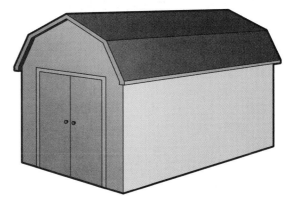

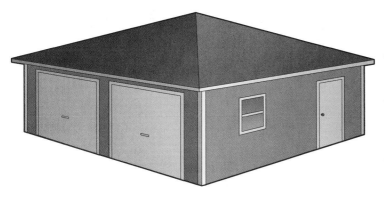

Hip. This roof slopes down from the top in four directions. Because the roof overhang runs around the entire perimeter, it offers the best protection against the elements for you and your structure. On the downside, the complex roofline is more difficult to frame, involving scores of compound miter cuts, and it offers less upstairs storage space than a gable or gambrel roof.

To Match or Not to Match?

Siding, roofing, windows, and other finish materials will establish your shed's personality. There are two roads to travel here. One is to have the structure blend in with existing structures as much as possible by using similar materials and matching the rooflines. The other option is to ignore the style and design of existing structures completely.

Have you always yearned for a Victorian house? Then how about a Victorian shed? What about an Arts and Crafts artist's studio? Virtually any style can be mimicked by identifying its trademark architectural features and applying them to your structure. Or maybe you prefer an eclectic shed made exclusively from recycled "found objects." Some homeowners like to think of their outbuildings as conversation pieces—it's all a matter of personal preference.

To get some ideas for the look of your structure, drive around town and note any buildings that strike your fancy. Likewise, page through home magazines and this book for ideas. Try to identify what it is about each structure that you like. Is it the color scheme? The roofline? The scrolled trimwork? Maybe it's the surrounding patio. The better you define what you like, the easier it'll be to settle on a final look.

ABOVE: This tiny shed makes a big statement with bright red paint, impeccable trim, and iron strap hinges on its green door. RIGHT: A handsome woodshed combines rustic style with rustic materials; the hip roof and siding, both of untrimmed rough-sawn pine, recall early hand-hewn American structures. OPPOSITE: Here, it's all about color. Primaries provide a blast of energy to both the shed-roofed greenhouse and its surroundings.

OPPOSITE, TOP: Red doors add traditional punch to the classic gray sidings—horizontal near the door, vertical on the sides, and shingled inside the front eyebrow overhang. The concrete foundation includes a 6-foot slab extension in front that's ringed by gravel. OPPOSITE, BOTTOM: Three wood stains highlight the craftsmanship of this handsome barn, customized from a kit. Note the striking multiplaned roofline, too.

A modern take on the shed-roof style includes painted fiber-cement siding, double French doors, and a raised roof "lid" of galvanized metal with glazed transoms below. This shed meets the adjacent patio via a raised brick landing.

CUSTOM TOUCHES

IN BUILDING, AS IN LIFE, IT'S THE LITTLE THINGS THAT COUNT. Sheds and garages themselves are pretty basic, but the following amenities can turn yours into something special—a model of efficiency or a stylish garden focal point.

- **EXTERIOR TRIM.** Decorative touches like window trim and roof fascia go a long way toward customizing your shed. For style pointers, see pages 24–29.
- **WINDOWS AND DOORS.** Picture windows, sliding or Dutch doors, and ganged skylights can make a cold, dark shed or garage light and airy. For shopping tips, see pages 52–53.
- **INTERIOR FINISH.** Wall coverings, floor coverings, window trim, and other interior treatments transform a basic shed into a little house. For pointers, see pages 54–55. Insulation not only helps trap heat in winter but also keeps things cooler in summer.

ABOVE: Bright splashes of paint on windows and siding set off a hanging collection of old garden tools.

It's the fine points—like trim, siding, shutters, cupola, and picket fence—that change this garden shed into a classic cottage. Trellises allow roses to scramble up the structure and wave their heads in the breeze.

BELOW: This potter's studio includes lots of custom touches: sliding barn doors, scrollwork, gable glazing, and exterior wainscoting made from log rounds embedded in mortar. The heartwood Douglas fir was reclaimed from an old mill; the roofing is fired ceramic tiles. A birdhouse perches above the doors.

• STORAGE STRATEGIES. Wall racks, shelves, cabinets, and even built-in cabinets and benches allow a simple floor plan to work harder. For ideas, see pages 154–159.

• HARDSCAPE. Decking, paving, paths, stairs, and ramps help lead the way to your new shed or garage. How about a built-in seating area, an arbor, or a privacy screen?

• LANDSCAPE. Want to blend your new structure into the existing land-scape? Surround it with plants in beds, raised planters, and containers to soften its edges. Hide mundane shed or garage walls with attached trellises, window boxes, and espaliered vines or roses.

• INDOOR AND OUTDOOR LIGHTING. An office, a studio, or a guesthouse needs a little interior lighting at night. Overhead tracks, pendants, or floor lamps can fill the bill; more contemplative spaces might simply call for candles or an oil lantern. And don't forget outdoor fixtures. Path lights lead the way; uplights and downlights add accents; rope lights mark steps; and floodlights add security to a remote site. Place outdoor circuits on a timer, daylight sensor, or motion sensor for hands-free control.

OPPOSITE: Formal as can be, the focal point of this cottage garden is its strikingly detailed potting shed. Shingles, cupola, porch, and pickets make the style; border plantings tie it to the surrounding garden.

ABOVE: A slew of recycled windows forms a greenhouse shed with multiple roof planes. LEFT: The patio hardscape and inset plantings link this shed to its sur-roundings. Arched trellises and climbing vines soften the otherwise blank exterior.

OPPOSITE: Shed interiors offer as many decorating options as their outsides. Here, the bare-bones wall studs and siding are dressed with glass-block glazing, a brick-and-barnwood floor, a twig chair, and a collection of plants and artwork to create a highly personalized space.

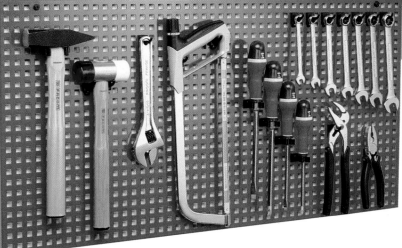

ABOVE: Though they've been used in store displays for years, a growing number of companies are now making "slotwall" panels suitable for the walls of sheds and garages. Shelves, baskets, hooks, and even cabinets hang from the grooved panels. LEFT: Remember good ol' pegboard? It's back—updated in colorful, durable steel.

LEFT: Built from recycled wood and wire screening, a roomy potting bench offers plenty of counter space as well as open areas above and below for storage. A brightly stenciled paint job gives it personality. Note the additional creative details, including hanging tiered baskets, a scale, and whimsical garden collectibles. Except for the weatherproof metal doors and the acrylic roofing, only recycled construction materials were used. The "floor" is a crunchy layer of practical pea gravel.

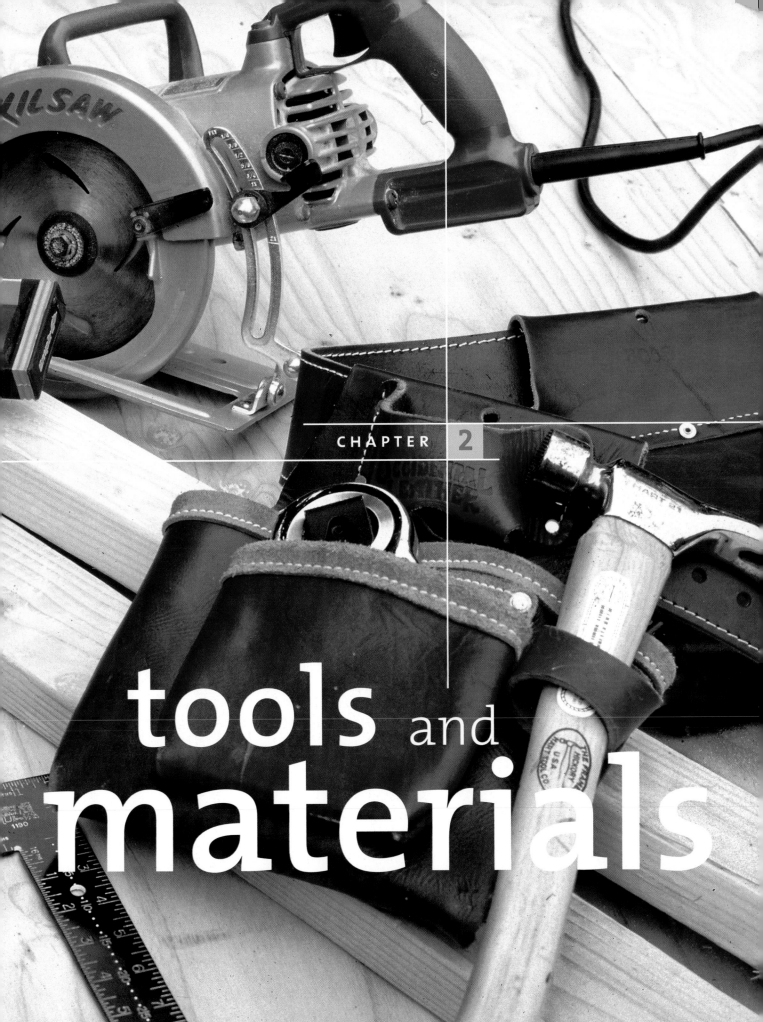

tools and materials

HAND TOOLS

READY TO BUILD A SHED? First you'll need some tools. Hand tools are a carpenter's traditional tools of choice; power tools (described on pages 42–43) are becoming more affordable all the time and can help the work go faster.

A collection of basic hand tools is outlined below. You may already have some or all of these tools, but if you're shopping, this information can point you in the right direction.

- **STEEL MEASURING TAPE.** To lay out your project with precision, you'll need a tape measure for general purpose measuring (and for larger structures, you may want a 50-foot reel tape as well). A simple 12-foot tape may be all you need for a small lean-to shed, but for larger jobs consider a ¾- or 1-inch-wide tape that's 16 or 25 feet long. These wider tapes won't twist and buckle, so you can extend them over longer distances.

Tape
measure

- **SQUARE.** A square helps you draw straight lines across lumber to be cut; it also helps check angles on assembled pieces of the structure. The speed square is the carpenter's staple square. A larger, 16- by 24-inch framing square is useful when laying out roof rafters and checking square over longer distances. The stouter the square, the less likely it is to get bent out of shape.

Speed square

Framing square

- **CROSSCUT SAW.** Even if you have a power saw, it's nice to keep a handsaw nearby to finish notches or cut in awkward spots. Unlike the specialized ripsaw (used for "ripping" wood with the grain), a crosscut saw is designed to cut boards across their widths; it's also handy for cutting plywood. A 26-inch blade with 8 points per inch is a good choice.

Crosscut saw

● **COMPASS SAW.** With a compass saw or the closely related jab saw, you can make quick cutouts in wood or gypsum wallboard (drywall). Some models feature a replaceable blade, which is handy when you bend the original.

Jab saw

Framing hammer

● **CLAW HAMMER.** Most carpenters use a light curved-claw hammer for finish work and a heavier straight-claw model for framing (it packs a bigger wallop for longer nails). Hammers have either smooth or serrated faces. The smooth face can minimize any dings you might make in the wood, but a serrated ("waffle") face is often the choice for rough framing because it won't slide off the nail as easily. Hammers range from about 13 to 28 ounces; in general, choose the heaviest hammer you can comfortably wield.

Finish hammer

● **LEVEL.** To check that things are on a true horizontal (level) or a true vertical (plumb), you'll need a level or two. The longer it is, the greater its accuracy will be. A carpenter's level is typically 2 feet long; a 4-foot mason's level is even better if you've got the space to use it. A small torpedo level is handy in tight quarters; simply tuck one into your tool belt.

Carpenter's level

To check level across longer distances, consider a line level or a water level (essentially a water-filled tube); new electronic versions emit a beep when the levels at both ends line up.

Water level

Torpedo level

● **PLUMB BOB.** Nothing but a pointed weight at the end of a string, the plumb bob provides a foolproof way to gauge plumb—by gravity. The plumb bob is especially good for transferring overhead points to the ground or floor below, or vice versa.

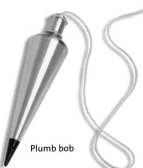

Plumb bob

• **CHALK LINE.** This long, spool-wound cord is housed within a case of powdered, colored chalk; it's great for both marking long cutting lines on sheet materials and laying out reference lines on a wall, ceiling, or floor. The type with a pointed case can double as a plumb bob.

Chalk line

Utility knife

• **UTILITY KNIFE.** Keep one of these handy for cutting and scribing tasks; pick one with retractable, replaceable blades. The new folding type shown is safest; it opens and closes like a pocketknife.

Block plane

• **CHISEL, BLOCK PLANE.** Though not really essential, these basic carpenter's tools are handy for cleaning up errant saw cuts and joints. The plastic-handled, metal-capped butt chisel can be driven with a hammer. Both planes and chisels are useless unless they're sharp, so you'll want to add a sharpening stone to your kit, too.

Butt chisel

• **PRY BAR.** Made a mistake or need to undo some old work? Consider the pry bar, which typically has a claw at one end and an angle at the other that can be driven by a hammer. The bigger the bar, the more leverage you'll have, but small pry bars are better for digging out small nails.

Pliers

• **PLIERS.** A pair of 9- or 10-inch lineman's pliers with wire cutters will twist and cut wire and pull out errant fasteners. Locking pliers are another useful tool.

Pry bar

• **WRENCHES.** An adjustable wrench is good for many bolt or nut sizes but not as precise as a box or open-end wrench. A ratchet-and-socket set may be required to reach into a countersunk bolt hole.

Adjustable wrenches

- **CLAMPS.** When you feel like you need an extra pair of hands, what you really need is a clamp. Clamps hold things where you want them; they're also essential for holding some parts together while the glue dries. C-clamps are the old standby, but bar clamps have a longer reach. The spring clamp, which looks like an oversize clothespin, is inexpensive and great for small jobs.

Bar clamp

Spring clamp

Play It Safe

As with any home improvement project, it's important to protect yourself by wearing appropriate safety gear.

- Respiratory protection keeps you from inhaling harmful vapors, dust, or fibers. For vapors or fine particles, use a respirator with interchangeable filters designed for specific applications. Disposable dust masks are sufficient for heavy sawdust.
- Ear protection is crucial for work with power tools. Earmuff protectors and lightweight foam earplugs filter excess noise but allow you to hear.
- To guard your hands, wear all-leather or leather-reinforced cotton work gloves when handling rough lumber—especially pressure-treated wood. Use rubber or plastic gloves for work with solvents, finishes, or adhesives.

Earmuffs

Earplugs

Gloves

Respirator

Safety goggles

Dust mask

- To protect your eyes, wear a full-face shield, safety glasses, or safety goggles any time your work might send dust and debris flying. Look for a comfortably fitted, fog-free type made of shatterproof plastic.
- Finally, consider protective headgear whenever working in tight quarters or with overhead framing members. This kind of work can involve a lot of kneeling, so you might also appreciate a pair of knee pads.
- If you'll be working with power tools, shock-resistant double-insulated tools and a GFCI-protected extension cord are worthwhile investments.

POWER TOOLS

THE FOLLOWING PORTABLE POWER TOOLS can make shed projects go a lot faster, and in the hands of the average do-it-yourselfer they produce better results than hand tools. Big, expensive stationary power tools can also be had, and if you have access to a table saw, band saw, or radial-arm saw in particular, you'll find they're great for some stages of shed building.

Cordless drill

Twist bit

Spade bit

Phillips-head bit

Star-drive bit

Hole saw

● ELECTRIC DRILL AND BITS. This power tool has all but replaced hand drills and screwdrivers (at least when more than a couple of screws are involved). For general tasks, look for a 3/8-inch reversible drill; cordless models are very handy. To bore holes up to 1/2 inch in diameter, use standard twist bits; for larger holes, use spade bits or a hole saw. A carbide-tipped masonry bit can tackle brick or stucco. When fitted with a Phillips-head or star-drive bit, the drill is equally handy as a power screwdriver, but you'll need a variable-speed model to keep from stripping screws. Models that have an adjustable clutch prevent screws from being driven too deep.

Use an electric drill with a 1/2-inch chuck for large-diameter holes—or even for mixing joint compound. Depending on your structure, you may also need a right-angle drill for working in tight spots or a hammer drill with a concrete bit for drilling into concrete. (You can rent both these tools as required.)

● PORTABLE CIRCULAR SAW. The circular saw does the same job as a handsaw, but much more quickly. When fitted with a carbide-tipped combination blade, it handles both crosscuts and rip cuts. The 7 1/4-inch size is standard. Worm-drive models are generally strongest, and the position of the motor housing allows you to see the cutting line while you cut.

Circular saw

Reciprocating saw

- **RECIPROCATING SAW.** Not only is this power saw the number-one demolition tool, it's also great for cutting out window and door openings in sheathing as well as cutting through sill plates at doors. Just don't use one where you need a straight, clean finish cut—try the circular saw or jigsaw instead.

- **JIGSAW (SABER SAW).** This is the electric version of the traditional coping saw; it can be used for both straight and delicately curved cuts. Unlike a coping saw, the jigsaw can make cuts well away from an edge, and it even makes interior "pocket" cuts if you drill an access hole first. Choose the right blades for different tasks: thin, fine-toothed blades for tight curves, beefier ones for rougher, straight cuts. A variable-speed model allows you to match the speed to the job.

Jigsaw

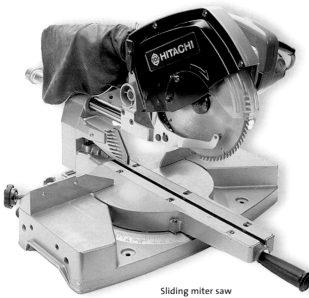

Sliding miter saw

- **POWER MITER SAW.** The pivoting power miter saw, or "chop saw," is the best choice for making precise crosscuts and angled cuts in trim. In addition, it cuts framing members to length with precision. A 10-inch miter saw is standard. So-called compound miter saws cut angles in two directions at once, a feature that's sometimes handy for rafters or profiled trim. Sliding miter saws can cut stock up to about 12 inches wide. Consider renting one of these tools for a day or two if you don't already own one.

- **NAIL GUN.** These replacements for the humble hammer come in a number of versions, including framing nailers, finish nailers, and staple guns. You'll need a compressor and an air hose to drive these tools. You certainly don't need a nail gun to build your shed, but if you have access to one, it can make jobs like nailing roofing or sheathing go much faster.

Finish nailer

Framing nailer

LUMBER AND HARDWARE

LUMBER, FASTENERS, AND FRAMING CONNECTORS are the basic blocks that your shed or garage will be built from. By understanding your options, you'll save both time and money. Need more info on shed-building terms and construction? Take a look at Chapter Three, "Building Basics," beginning on page 56.

Lumberyard Lingo

For starters, lumber is divided into softwoods and hardwoods. These terms refer to the origin of the wood: softwoods come from conifers, hardwoods from deciduous trees. As a rule, softwoods are much less expensive and more readily available than hardwoods.

Wall studs and other framing members are typically 2 by 4s or 2 by 6s. In the East, a softwood group called SFP (spruce-fir-pine) is most commonly used. In the West, Douglas fir or hem-fir is standard. Douglas fir is the strongest of all these types and is often used for framing members that will be stressed, such as floor joists or roof rafters.

Pressure-treated Lumber

Though redwood and cedar heartwoods are naturally resistant to decay and termites, most other woods soon rot and weaken if they come into prolonged contact with soil or water. To solve this problem, less durable types of lumber (such as Southern pine and Western hem-fir) are often factory-treated with chemical preservatives that guard against rot, insects, and other sources of decay. These woods are less expensive than redwood or cedar, and in some areas they're more readily available.

Pressure-treated wood is available in two "exposures." For lumber that will be close to the ground, the Ground Contact type is required. Use the Above Ground type for other applications.

Working with treated lumber has its drawbacks. The primary preservative used in pressure-treated lumber contains toxic metals. As a precaution, wear safety glasses and a dust mask when cutting this type of lumber, and wear gloves when handling it for prolonged periods. And never burn the scraps.

Douglas fir

Hem-fir

Pressure-treated fir

Pine

Preprimed pine

Redwood

Framing lumber is rated for strength. The most common grading system, from best to worst, includes the grades Select Structural, No. 1, No. 2, and No. 3. Lumberyards often sell a mix of grades called No. 2 and Better. Other grading systems used for some lumber (typically 2 by 4s) classify wood according to the grades Construction, Standard, and Utility or as a mixture of grades called Standard or Better. The higher the grade, the more you'll have to pay. One of the best ways to save money on a project is to identify and use the most appropriate—not the costliest—grade for each element.

For lumber that's directly exposed to the elements, consider pressure-treated lumber (see the facing page) to resist damage from insects and moisture. Redwood and cedar heartwood (the darker part of the wood, from the tree's core) are naturally immune to those threats but cost significantly more—and they don't offer the strength of pine or fir.

Remember that lumber sizes are designated before the wood is surface planed and are not true dimensions. The finished size of a 2 by 4, for example, is actually about $1\frac{1}{2}$ by $3\frac{1}{2}$ inches. Likewise, a 4 by 4 is actually about $3\frac{1}{2}$ by $3\frac{1}{2}$ inches. Other actual sizes are listed at right.

The least expensive lumber you'll find at home centers is "green" wood, which was not dried before surfacing. Green wood can shrink, twist, and split once it's installed, causing problems. For best results, consider slightly pricier KD (kiln-dried) or air-dried lumber, if you can find it.

LUMBER	DIMENSIONS
1 by 3	$\frac{3}{4}$ by $2\frac{1}{2}$ inches
1 by 4	$\frac{3}{4}$ by $3\frac{1}{2}$ inches
2 by 4	$1\frac{1}{2}$ by $3\frac{1}{2}$ inches
2 by 6	$1\frac{1}{2}$ by $5\frac{1}{2}$ inches
2 by 8	$1\frac{1}{2}$ by $7\frac{1}{4}$ inches
4 by 4	$3\frac{1}{2}$ by $3\frac{1}{2}$ inches

Plywood sheathing

Tongue-and-groove subflooring

Oriented strand board

Sheathing

Sheathing is the skin that covers framing members. Today, sheathing means sheet products. Two basic types are available: plywood and oriented strand board (or OSB), usually in 4- by 8-foot panels.

Floor sheathing or subflooring has tongue-and-groove edges that interlock. It's typically ¾ inch thick but can sometimes be as thick as $1\frac{1}{8}$ inches. Exterior wall sheathing is usually ½- or ⅝-inch-thick plywood or OSB. Roof decking is most commonly ⅝-inch plywood.

All sheathing should be span rated. The rating looks like a fraction (such as $^{32}/_{16}$), but it isn't. The upper number describes the maximum spacing of supports in inches when the panel is used for roof sheathing; the lower number denotes the maximum support spacing when applied as subflooring.

Fasteners

Nails, screws, and bolts are the "glue" that hold your shed together. Here's how to choose the right ones for the job.

● NAILS. When joining framing members unexposed to weather, use vinyl- or cement-coated sinkers. These are coated with a dry adhesive and won't later work their way out. Use hot-dipped galvanized or stainless steel nails for applying exposed siding and trim.

As far as type of nail goes, you can use common or finish nails. Heavy-duty common nails have a head and a thick shank—a feature that makes them more difficult to drive but increases their holding power. Choose a finish nail when the head shouldn't show; drive it nearly flush, then sink the rounded head with a nailset.

Standard nail sizes are given in "pennies," abbreviated as "d" (from the Latin *denarius,* a type of Roman coin). The higher the penny number, the longer the nail. Equivalents in inches for the most frequently used nails are as follows:

3d = $1\frac{1}{4}$ inches	8d = $2\frac{1}{2}$ inches
4d = $1\frac{1}{2}$ inches	10d = 3 inches
6d = 2 inches	16d = $3\frac{1}{2}$ inches

Choose nails about twice as long as the thickness of the material you'll be nailing through. Most shed framing is secured with 8d and 16d nails.

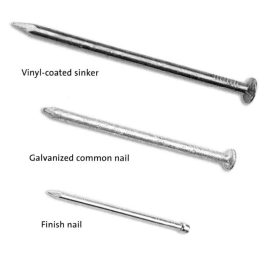

Vinyl-coated sinker

Galvanized common nail

Finish nail

• SCREWS. Though they're more expensive than nails, coated or stainless steel outdoor screws offer several advantages. They don't pop out as readily as nails, they're less likely to be damaged during installation, and since they aren't pounded in, you don't have to worry about hammer dents or pieces moving while you hammer.

Deck screws are surprisingly easy to drive into softwoods if you use an electric drill or screw gun with an adjustable clutch and a screwdriver bit. Drywall screws come in smaller sizes than deck screws but are less weather resistant. The heavy-duty lag screw has a square or hexagonal head and must be tightened with a wrench.

Choose screws that are long enough to penetrate about twice the top member's thickness (for example, use $2\frac{1}{2}$- or 3-inch screws to join 2 by 4s or 2 by 6s).

• BOLTS. For heavy-duty fastening, choose bolts. The machine bolt has a square or hexagonal head, two washers, and a nut; it must be tightened with a wrench at each end. The carriage bolt has a self-anchoring head that digs into the wood as the nut is tightened. Expanding anchors allow you to secure wooden members to a masonry wall.

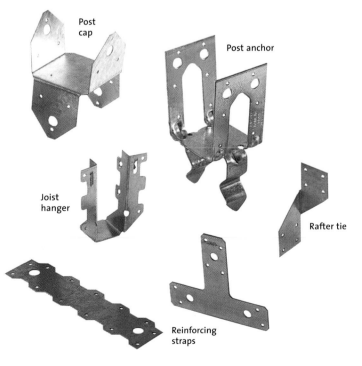

Drywall screw · Stainless steel screw · Deck screw · Lag screw · Machine bolt · Carriage bolt · Washer · Nut · Expanding anchors

Framing Connectors

Many building codes require galvanized metal framing hardware where floor joists meet headers or rim joists, where studs meet sole plates, and so on. Check with your building inspector to identify what type of connectors (if any) are required in your area.

Even where they're not required, connectors can add strength and help prevent lumber splits caused by toenailing (page 71) two boards together. Connectors handy for shed building include joist hangers, post anchors, post caps, rafter ties, hurricane ties, and a variety of reinforcing straps. Be sure to attach them with the nails specified by the manufacturer; they are shorter and fatter than standard nails.

Post cap · Post anchor · Joist hanger · Rafter tie · Reinforcing straps

ROOFING MATERIALS

ROOFING MATERIALS VARY WIDELY in appearance, durability, and ease of installation. Sheds and garages lend themselves to asphalt shingles, while larger barns often use metal roofing. Regardless of the material used, all these structures need flashing to protect and seal the roof.

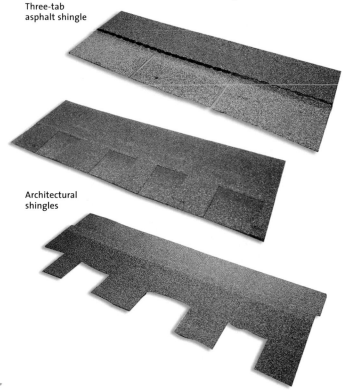

Three-tab asphalt shingle

Architectural shingles

● ASPHALT SHINGLES. These are the most common roofing material, as they're inexpensive, long lasting (some brands up to 40 years), and available in a wide variety of colors and textures. The 12- by 36-inch shingles cover large areas quickly and are a snap to cut and nail. They're suitable for any climate but should be used only on roofs with at least a 4-in-12 slope (page 74).

The two main styles are three-tab and architectural. Standard three-tab shingles have evenly spaced slots; architectural types are laminated from two layers and have wider, random notches, which add depth and texture once installed.

● WOOD SHINGLES AND SHAKES. Shingles are sawn from chunks of Western red cedar and have a smooth, finished appearance. Cedar shakes are thicker and rougher, and are usually split by hand or machine. Both shingles and shakes weigh less than asphalt shingles and can better withstand the freeze-thaw cycles common in cold climates. On the down side, they're expensive and time-consuming to install. In some areas, they're banned due to fire danger.

Though shingles are available in several grades (suitable for siding as well as roofing), it's best to specify Number 1 ("Blue Label") for use on a roof.

Cedar shake

Cedar shingle

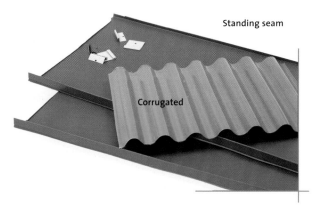

Standing seam

Corrugated

● METAL ROOFING. Corrugated and standing-seam metal roofing are excellent choices for large buildings such as barns. In the past, these roofing materials were installed only by pros and were quite expensive. Today, there are economical snap-together systems designed for the average homeowner. Some metal roofing is coated with baked-on enamel or even vinyl. Because metal roofing expands and contracts with heat and cold, flexible fasteners must be used to keep the fastener holes sealed.

● PLASTICS. Clear or translucent glazing is another option. PVC and fiberglass are old standbys that come in flat or corrugated versions.

Acrylic and polycarbonate are lightweight updates and have the highest light transmission of all plastic glazing. They're both available in single- and double-wall panels. Double (or "twin") panels provide greater insulation and admit about 80 percent of available light.

Polycarbonate is also available in triple-wall panels—particularly popular for potting sheds and greenhouses—and in textured and translucent versions. Polycarbonate expands and shrinks, so you'll need special fasteners; panels can be joined with custom clips and channels.

● FLASHING. Protect exposed seams and openings by adding flashing to your structure. It can be made of galvanized sheet metal, aluminum, copper, rubber, or plastic. Metal flashing is available in rolls that you can cut and bend yourself. Typical flashing includes drip edge to cover the ends of eaves and gables; vent collars, which seal the openings around vents; Z-flashing, which seals above windows and doors; and step flashing, used along walls, dormers, and chimneys. To secure the flashing, use fasteners made of the same material. This prevents a chemical reaction that can produce corrosion.

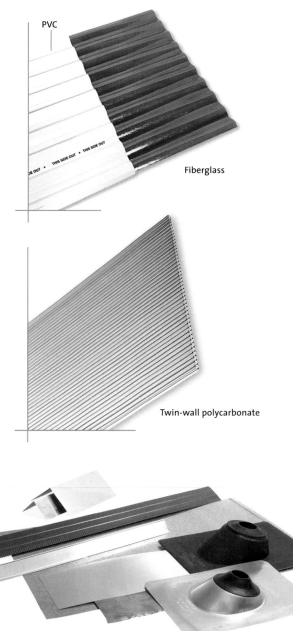

PVC

Fiberglass

Twin-wall polycarbonate

Flashing

SIDING

THE OUTER LAYER OF YOUR WALLS is every bit as important as the roof in protecting your backyard structure from the weather. But siding offers more than protection. The materials you choose do much to create the "look" of your structure.

Popular siding materials for sheds, garages, and barns include solid wood boards, exterior plywood, and fiber-cement. Other options include vinyl and aluminum, though both can require special tools and are best installed by pros. And don't forget corrugated aluminum sheets for that funky industrial-chic look.

Preprimed pine channel

Laminated (composite) shiplap

Tongue-and-groove pine

Redwood V-rustic

Preprimed cedar bevel

● WOOD SIDING. Some sheds and barns call for traditional board siding or wood shingles (page 48). The best boards are typically either redwood or cedar, though if you're painting you'll save a lot of money by buying pine instead. Popular profiles include clapboard or bevel, channel, shiplap, V-rustic, and tongue and groove. You can also buy square-edge boards and cover the joints between them with narrow battens (page 83). Some profiles are best installed vertically; others can run horizontally.

Board texture is either smooth or rough-sawn. Rough-sawn lumber has a texture that's rustic yet not too bumpy, and it accepts stains beautifully.

● PLYWOOD. Plywood sheet siding goes up fast and won't require separate wall sheathing (page 46) beneath it. You could simply buy exterior-grade plywood, but the almost universal siding choice is the ubiquitous grooved sheet known as T1-11. It's available in plain, rough-sawn, and preprimed versions, almost always with vertical grooves spaced on 4- or 8-inch centers. Standard plywood size is 4 by 8 feet, though 9- and 10-foot panels can be ordered.

T1-11 plywood

● FIBER-CEMENT. For the look of wood without the maintenance hassles, a lot of people are opting for fiber-cement siding. Fiber-cement is a mixture of Portland cement, sand, and cellulose fibers. It comes in both "board" and sheet sizes. The clapboard-style boards run 5 to 12 inches wide; sheets come plain or grooved. Both types take paint well and are resistant to fire, rot, and insects.

On the downside, fiber-cement is heavy and harder to nail than wood. Cutting it with standard tools produces billowing clouds of dust; it's best to rent special shears or a snap cutter instead.

Fiber-cement

Paint and Stain Portfolio

A fine finish will protect your shed while offering almost unlimited decorative potential. Suitable products include paints, stains, and water sealers. Here's a closer look at each option.

EXTERIOR PAINT. Both oil- and water-based (latex) paints come in flat, low-luster, semigloss, and high-gloss finishes. Shed siding is usually painted with a flat finish, and trim in low luster or semigloss for durability. In most cases, latex is the paint of choice—it's fast drying and easy to clean up with soap and water.

Paints can be custom-mixed to any color, or you can choose from a wide array of standard colors. Paint companies often offer preselected palettes to help coordinate trim and siding. Wood should always be painted with a coat of primer before the finish coat is applied.

EXTERIOR STAIN. Stains may be semitransparent or solid color (opaque). The former contain enough pigment to tint the wood surface but not enough to mask the grain; they produce a natural, informal look. Solid-color stains are essentially paints; their heavy pigments cover the wood grain completely.

Under most conditions, semitransparent stain has a shorter life span than either paint or solid-color stain.

WATER SEALER. Applied to unfinished wood, clear sealers won't color the wood but will darken it slightly. You can buy them in oil- and water-based versions. Many formulations include both UV-blockers and mildewcides to protect wood; some come in slightly tinted versions. Like semitransparent stains, sealers allow you to show off wood that has a beautiful grain and color, but they do need to be renewed frequently.

WINDOWS AND DOORS

MODERN WINDOWS AND DOORS make it easy to add light, access, and personality to your shed or garage. Manufactured windows feature energy-efficient double-insulated panes and tough coatings. Exterior doors have evolved as well, with steel and fiberglass challenging solid-wood versions. If your structure needs extra light, consider skylights, too.

Windows

Windows come in almost unlimited shapes, and you can even gang various shapes and sizes to create a window wall. Most basic styles—like fixed, casement, sliding, or double-hung—are available as standard orders from home improvement centers or companies that specialize in windows. Or you can custom-order special shapes, sizes, and kinds of glass—at a price, of course.

Frames may be wood, wood with vinyl or aluminum cladding, aluminum, vinyl, steel, or fiberglass. Wood has the advantage of being paintable in any color, but cladding (available in a range of colors) eliminates most exterior maintenance problems. Aluminum—the least expensive alternative—is low maintenance but stylistically more limited. Vinyl, another inexpensive choice, is virtually maintenance-free, though colors are usually limited to white and gray; fiberglass is similar but varies in quality. Durable steel, the most expensive choice, is excellent for clean, contemporary styling.

Vinyl sliding window

High-tech Help

Double-glazing, or insulating glass made of two panes of glass sealed together with space between, can go a long way toward preventing heat loss. The newer *low-e* (low-emissivity) glass adds a coating that reduces indoor heat loss in cold weather and keeps ultraviolet rays out—which helps prevent fading of furnishings. Tinted glass can also block solar heat gain to help keep things comfortably cool in hot weather.

Doors

Traditional exterior doors are either frame-and-panel solid wood or flush (flat) plywood skins with solid wood cores. But take a look at steel or fiberglass, too. Besides offering better fire protection, these materials are usually better insulated and won't expand and contract like wood, and their tough exteriors stand up well to constant use and abuse. Prehung units include the door, the surrounding jambs, and premounted hinges. You simply place the unit in the framed opening and shim it level and plumb (page 85).

Besides standard exterior offerings, other doors suitable for backyard structures include patio doors (French or sliding), Dutch doors (with independent upper and lower sections), barn doors on overhead tracks, and roll-up garage-style doors.

You can, of course, also build your own door; for ideas, see page 84.

Prehung fiberglass door

Skylights

If you have privacy issues or want extra light and ventilation, skylights may be the answer. They're available in a range of sizes and styles, fixed and operable, and with or without screens. Consider placement carefully; a south-facing skylight can offer dramatic shifting light throughout the day but may let in too much light and heat, whereas a north-facing skylight usually provides soft, uniform light.

Curb-mounted skylight

Self-flashing skylight

Venting skylight

INTERIOR TRIM AND INSULATION

A RUSTIC SHED WON'T REQUIRE MUCH, if anything, in the way of interior finish. A working potting shed or wood shop calls for unfussy flooring and wall treatments that can take some hard knocks. At the other end of the spectrum, a live-in home office or guest cottage allows you to pull out all the stops. How about warming things up by insulating walls, ceiling, and/or floor? Here's a look at some interior options.

Fiberglass

Rigid foam

Cellulose

Insulation

Fiberglass insulation is inexpensive and offers R-values ranging from R-11 to R-35, depending on thickness. (An R-value rates resistance to heat transfer; the higher the number, the better.) It's available in widths designed to fit between studs and joists spaced 16 or 24 inches apart, as well as in other widths and with different backings. You can purchase rolls or precut lengths designed to fit in a standard wall. Unfaced insulation is press-fit between studs and joists without the use of fasteners. Faced insulation is pressed in place and then stapled. Fiberglass can irritate the skin, eyes, and lungs, so wear long pants, a long-sleeved shirt, gloves, goggles, and a dust mask.

Extruded polystyrene (or rigid foam) insulation is a dense foam board that generally offers around R-5 per inch of thickness. It's inexpensive and comes in 4- by 8-foot sheets or strips designed to fit between studs or joists spaced 16 or 24 inches apart. Sheets sometimes have tongue-and-groove edges so they can be joined together to create a continuous layer of insulation. Rigid foam can be press-fit in place or secured with construction adhesive or nails and screws.

Cellulose loose fill is commonly made from recycled paper combined with a flame retardant. Its R-value is similar to that of fiberglass—about R-3.5 per inch of thickness. Loose fill can be blown in and is an option for ceilings with low clearances where installing fiberglass would be difficult. However, it settles with age.

Wall Coverings

Interior walls can be left bare or covered. If you've added insulation, it's best to cover the walls to prevent damage to the insulation over time. Whatever material you decide on, make sure to have all inspections completed before closing in the walls.

Gypsum wallboard (drywall) is an economical and easy-to-install wall covering; ½- or ⅝-inch sheets will hold up better than thinner ones.

Another excellent option for covering interior walls is T1-11 plywood siding (page 50). Though more expensive than drywall, plywood siding can handle the day-to-day abuse the interior walls of an outbuilding get without showing dings or dents. You can also buy thinner plywood or hardboard panels made expressly for interior walls. Perforated hardboard, or pegboard, is another familiar option.

If you're planning on using your new building as living space, consider upgrading to solid wood paneling. It's available in many colors and patterns and goes up quickly with construction adhesive and/or nails.

Wallboard joint compound and tape

Pine shiplap

Gypsum wallboard

Pegboard

Plywood beadboard

Moldings

Moldings and Trim

Look for stock moldings at lumberyards or home centers, and special or custom patterns from molding and millwork shops. Paint-grade pine moldings, which have visible finger joints along their length, are much less expensive than stain-grade oak or other hardwoods that can be finished naturally. You can buy moldings either unfinished or coated with primer.

If you're painting, also take a look at moldings made from medium-density fiberboard. MDF takes paint very well, is less expensive than most wood moldings, and is less prone to warping than wood—especially in large profiles such as crown molding. Most MDF moldings come preprimed.

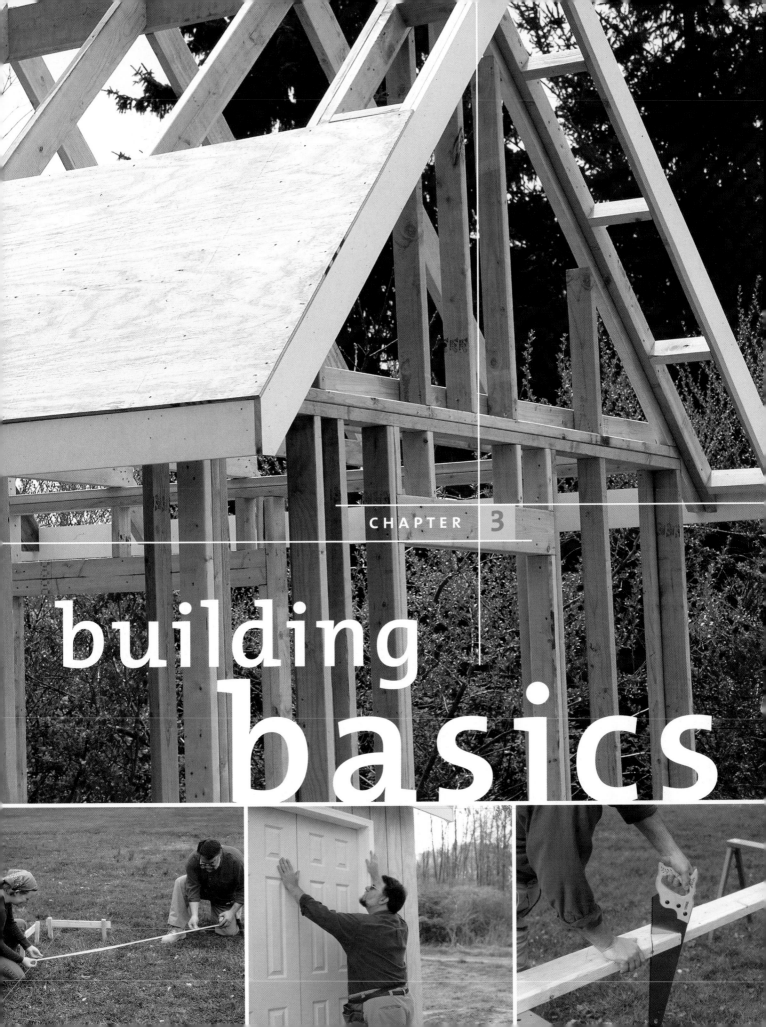

building
basics

THE BIG PICTURE

A SIMPLE SHED MAKES AN IDEAL PROJECT FOR A BUDDING CARPENTER. And while a garage or a barn is more demanding (particularly of the friends and family members you'll need as helpers), each allows a reasonable margin of error compared with residential remodeling projects. Best of all, these projects are built outdoors, where the havoc of construction won't disrupt daily life.

In addition to having fastening and cutting skills (especially the safe and accurate use of a circular saw), you will need to be comfortable making precise measurements and checking, again and again, that your work is level and plumb. You'll also need a framing square and a handy technique called the "3-4-5 triangle" (page 66) to verify that your work is square.

Whether exploring new techniques or refreshing old skills, you'll find that this chapter offers the essential construction know-how for successfully completing your shed, garage, or barn. For step-by-step projects, see Chapter Four, beginning on page 96. Or maybe you'd prefer a kit shed; for more information on those, see the box below.

The first step in building any structure is to have the building plans and site plan approved by your local building inspector. A small shed may not need a permit, but because garages and barns are typically larger than sheds, they normally require building permits and must be built to code. Ask what needs to be inspected and at what stages. When everything is approved, you can prepare the site and start gathering your materials.

Building a Kit Shed

If you like the idea of a new shed but would rather not build one from scratch, consider a kit shed (see page 159 for a list of kit manufacturers). There are two basic types of kits available: parts kits and prefabricated kits. With a parts kit, you get a set of plans and most (if not all) of the materials. You need only cut the pieces to size and assemble the shed.

With a prefabricated kit, sections come already assembled and fit together to form the floor, walls, and roof. For an additional fee, most kit manufacturers offer an assembly service and can dispatch a crew to put the shed together for you.

Some manufacturers will also customize their creations—or you can do that part yourself with paint, trim, windows and skylights, a cupola, an arbor, or an adjacent patio or deck.

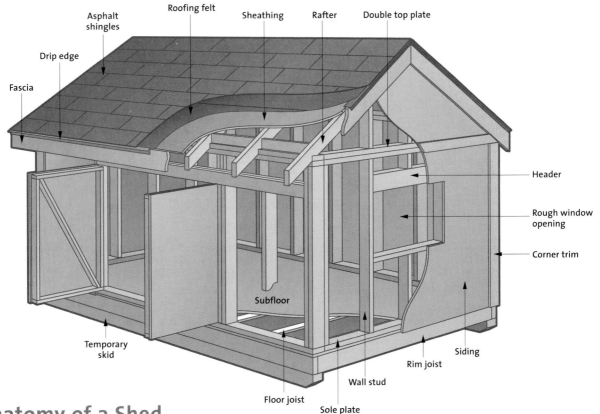

Asphalt shingles · Roofing felt · Sheathing · Rafter · Double top plate · Drip edge · Fascia · Header · Rough window opening · Corner trim · Subfloor · Temporary skid · Siding · Rim joist · Wall stud · Floor joist · Sole plate · Ridge board · Mudsill · Concrete slab

Anatomy of a Shed

Want to build a shed? First, take some time to learn about the basic building components and how they fit together.

A shed is built like a house—just smaller. Like a house, it rests on a foundation to give it a solid base. This can be temporary skids (shown above) or piers, poured footings, or a concrete slab (shown at right). Slabs double as floors; other foundations require separate floor platforms made from evenly spaced joists topped with structural sheathing.

The "stick-framed" walls are built from 2-by lumber in sections, then secured to the floor or slab and tied together above with double top plates. Rafters run between the top plates and a central ridge board and are typically sheathed with plywood (or in the case of wood roofs, with 1 by 4 boards). The sheathing is then covered with roofing felt and shingles or shakes. Windows and doors are installed in the rough openings, and the exterior walls are covered with sheathing and/or siding. Finally, trim is added for a finished look.

In sum, shed building follows a certain progression: foundation, flooring, walls, roofing, siding, windows and doors, and trim. These subjects are covered in order in the following sections, beginning on page 62.

Anatomy of a Garage

In many ways, garage construction is similar to that of a shed, but it requires stronger, stouter lumber—and more of it. Framing members need to be beefier to extend across longer distances or to accept thicker insulation. A wide structure may require 2 by 10s instead of 2 by 8s to span the walls without sagging. A garage built in the Midwest that also serves as a workshop will use 2 by 6s for the wall framing instead of 2 by 4s to hold the thicker fiberglass insulation needed in cold winters.

The foundation for the garage is usually some form of slab (page 63). Walls are typically built in sections and raised one at a time. They are braced upright temporarily and secured to the foundation with a mudsill that's attached with concrete anchors.

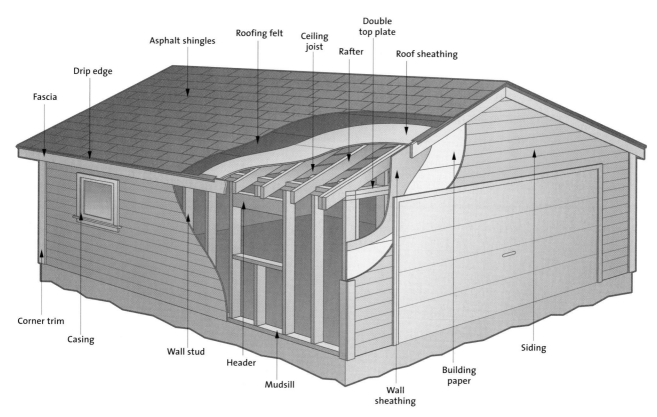

Rough openings are placed wherever doors or windows are to be installed, with headers at the top to support the weight of the roof. A large opening, like one for a garage door, requires a particularly beefy header. Ceiling joists span the walls and hold them together; rafters are attached to the ceiling joists and to the ridge board to form the roof. The rafters are covered with sheathing, roofing felt, and shingles or shakes. Windows and doors are installed, and exterior sheathing and/or siding is added, along with the exterior trim, to complete the garage.

Barn Basics

Because barns are often larger than garages and even houses, several alternative techniques are used for their construction. Besides stick framing, the most common are pole construction and timber framing.

Stick-framed barns are usually built on a slab foundation. Barn roofs are often built using premade trusses (page 75). The gambrel-style roof shown at right is a popular choice for barns, as it offers maximum storage space above.

A pole barn (shown below) is a quicker, less expensive way to build a barn. Poles are driven into the ground, and horizontal members called girts join the poles together. Vertical siding is then applied to enclose the space. Roof framing is simple, as rafters are secured to the girts at the top of the poles and to the ridge girt. The poles set into the ground can be round poles or square posts.

The beauty of pole construction is that no foundation is required. But that's not to say you can't add one—installing a framed floor above the ground is the best bet when flooding or pests are a concern.

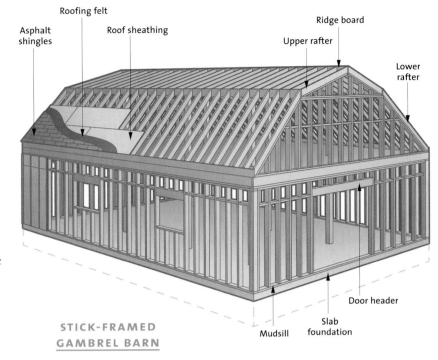

STICK-FRAMED GAMBREL BARN

Because no excavation is required, a pole barn is also the ideal choice for sloped sites.

If you want a barn that will last a lifetime and then some, consider using timber-framing construction. With this method, large, heavy timbers are connected using age-old techniques such as mortise and tenon joinery. The stout timbers span great distances and eliminate the need for wall studs. The downside? This is a job for the pros. Timber framing is a highly skilled craft and should not be attempted by anyone without training (there are a number of timber-framing schools nationwide).

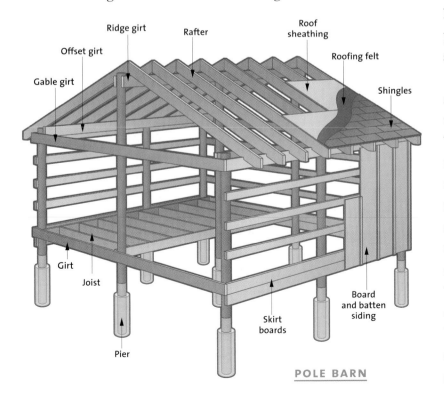

POLE BARN

FOUNDATIONS

IF THERE'S ONE PART OF BUILDING A SHED, GARAGE, OR BARN that's worth some extra time, it's creating a solid, square foundation. Small errors can telegraph into the finished structure, causing larger problems later.

A small shed can get by with only a pair of skids or a set of precast concrete piers as a foundation (see below). However, a larger shed requires a more permanent foundation with the structure attached to the concrete footing. Owing to their size and weight, garages and some barns are best built on slab foundations (see facing page).

Most shed foundations can be tackled by the average homeowner, but the slab foundation shown on pages 66–67 may call for professional help, as it requires deep footings, reinforcing rod (rebar) to prevent cracks, and a load or two from a cement mixer.

Temporary Foundations

A skid foundation is the easiest to build and move—the skids allow you to tow the shed to a new location if desired. Skids are typically made of pressure-treated 4 by 6s with the ends tapered to keep them from digging into the ground when moved. Even though the skids are pressure-treated, it's best to provide ample drainage to prevent rot. Excavate 4 inches of soil where the shed will be located. Then, to prevent weeds from growing under the shed, apply a layer of landscape cloth. Cover this with 4 inches of pea gravel. Good drainage also lessens the likelihood of soil eroding under a skid, causing the shed to tip.

Another way to make a temporary foundation is to use precast concrete piers or blocks. Some piers (like those shown below right) have notches in their tops to accept dimensional lumber. Like a skid foundation, a pier foundation needs ample drainage to remain stable. You can excavate the entire area or just small squares around each pier and fill in with pea gravel.

For either type of temporary foundation, the floor frame is built with 2-by joists, then covered with exterior-grade plywood. For details see pages 68–69.

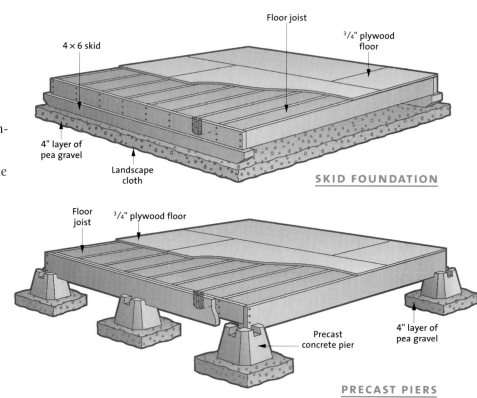

Floor joist

4 × 6 skid

³/₄" plywood floor

4" layer of pea gravel

Landscape cloth

SKID FOUNDATION

Floor joist

³/₄" plywood floor

Precast concrete pier

4" layer of pea gravel

PRECAST PIERS

Permanent Foundations

Permanent foundations can be poured footings, slabs, or T-shaped perimeter foundations that combine features of both. Some are designed for mild climates; freeze-proof versions guard against frost heave and cracking. Slab or T-shaped foundations typically are reinforced with rebar and/or wire mesh to help prevent shifting and cracking.

A poured footing is the simplest permanent foundation and is ideal for small structures like sheds. Because its base rests below the frost line, it's resistant to frost heave. Once the holes are dug, you can use concrete tube forms to shape the footings. The structure attaches to the footings with J-shaped anchor bolts and/or metal post bases embedded in the still-wet concrete.

An on-grade slab foundation is used in warm climates where there's no danger of the ground freezing and thereby expanding and cracking the concrete. It's made of several inches of concrete cast on a bed of crushed gravel and reinforced with wire mesh. A deeper trough or footing runs around the perimeter, reinforced with rebar.

A T-shaped foundation is an alternative for structures built in cold climates. This foundation consists of a footing that extends below the frost line, foundation walls that are centered over the footing, and sometimes a slab that runs between the walls. Footings are typically equal in depth to the width of the wall and twice as wide. Walls are made by pouring concrete into wood forms. Once the concrete is cured, the forms are removed.

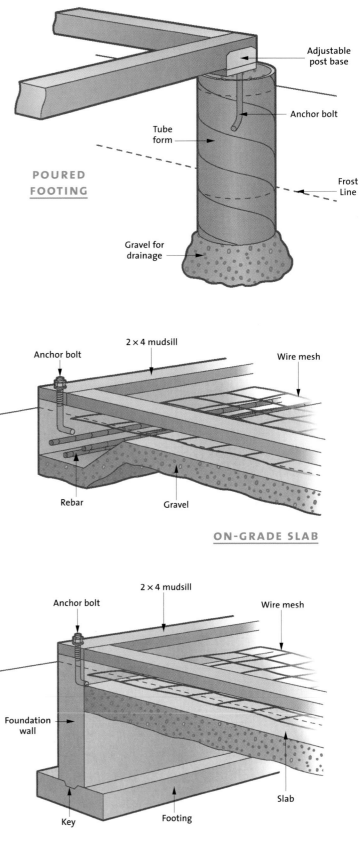

POURED FOOTING

Adjustable post base

Anchor bolt

Tube form

Frost Line

Gravel for drainage

ON-GRADE SLAB

Anchor bolt

2 × 4 mudsill

Wire mesh

Rebar

Gravel

T-SHAPED FOUNDATION

Anchor bolt

2 × 4 mudsill

Wire mesh

Foundation wall

Slab

Key

Footing

Installing a Temporary Foundation

Some projects call for movable footings like precast piers (page 62) or this even simpler design, which substitutes solid concrete blocks (4 by 8 by 16 inches). The blocks sit atop small tamped beds of pea gravel.

1 **DIG THE HOLES.** Lay out your foundation as detailed on page 66. Don't worry about being too precise; you'll fine-tune the layout later. Next, lay blocks in rough position according to your plan and spade around them to mark their locations. Then remove the blocks and dig a hole about 4 inches deep in each spot.

2 **PLACE AND LEVEL BLOCKS.** Fill each hole with pea gravel and tamp it down with a hand tamper or a wood block. Reposition the corner blocks, and check your layout by measuring diagonally from corner to corner; when the measurements match, the layout is square. Then check each block for level in both directions; use a small sledge or mallet to tap them into alignment. Don't worry yet about whether they're level to one another.

3 **LEVEL THE ROWS.** First bridge the end blocks in one row with a long, straight 2 by 4 and lay a level on top. Add or subtract some gravel and re-tamp or add half or full blocks atop the low ones as necessary. When the ends are level to one another, add and level any intermediate blocks.

Then bridge the end block of the row you just leveled with the end block of the second row, as shown at left. Again, add or subtract some gravel or add extra blocks as necessary. Finally, level the rest of this second row to the end block.

Installing Permanent Footings

Although you can dig holes for poured footings with a post-hole digger, a power auger (shown below) will do the job faster and without the backache. Most rental centers carry these—when you rent one, have the salesperson explain its operation. Caution: A power auger will kick when it bites into the dirt or hits a root or stone. It's best to have a helper assist you in holding the auger.

If you have more than a few bags of concrete to mix, you can rent a portable cement mixer, which will do the job quickly and with minimal effort on your part. Cement mixers are either gas or electric powered. If you rent an electric mixer, guard against shock by plugging it into a GFCI (ground fault circuit interrupter) receptacle.

1 DIG THE HOLES. First, lay out your foundation with batter boards and mason's line, as described on page 66. Your local code will specify how deep the frost line is and how far below it you need to dig (usually 12 inches). In most cases, codes will require you to provide drainage by adding a layer of gravel below the footings. If using concrete tube forms, cut them so they're 2 inches above grade when placed in the holes.

2 MIX AND POUR CONCRETE. Pour pre-mixed concrete into a wheelbarrow and make a depression in the center. Add the recommended amount of clean water and mix using a mortar hoe or shovel, moving the concrete back and forth until all the water is absorbed by the mix. Then slowly shovel the concrete into the holes. Large air bubbles trapped in the concrete can weaken it. Use a thin scrap of wood to poke the concrete and release any trapped air. Then draw a wood scrap over the forms to level, or "screed," the concrete.

3 INSTALL ANCHORS. Reposition the mason's lines on the batter boards and use a plumb bob to mark the anchor location in each footing. Push an anchor into the wet concrete and wiggle it to get the concrete to fill in around it. Adjust its position so the anchor is directly centered under the plumb bob, then use a torpedo level to check that the anchor is level and plumb.

Pouring a Slab Foundation

The on-grade slab foundation shown here is designed for mild conditions. In severe climates you'll need a T-shaped foundation (page 63) with perimeter footings that extend below the frost line. Be sure to check exact requirements in your area; you may also need a building permit.

Small slabs are fairly straightforward to install, although leveling and smoothing the surface require some special tools and skills. Larger foundations are best installed by professionals, as they may require deep footings, extensive formwork, reinforcement, and several loads from a cement mixer.

1 **LAY OUT THE FOUNDATION.** First consult your shed plan and roughly mark the corners of the footings with temporary stakes. Then position pairs of batter boards (pointed 2 by 4s driven into the ground and spanned with 1 by 4s) at right angles to each other about 18 inches behind each corner. Stretch mason's line between corners and use a 3-4-5 triangle (see below) to make sure the lines are perpendicular. Secure the lines as shown with nails driven into the batter boards.

3–4–5 Triangle

One of the oldest and most reliable ways to check adjacent legs of a corner for 90 degrees is to use a 3–4–5 triangle. To do this, measure and mark a point 3 feet from a corner where the lines cross, marking on either line. Then measure and mark 4 feet from the center point on the other line. Now measure the hypotenuse—the distance between the 3-foot mark and the 4-foot mark—with a tape measure (or a piece of string or wire rope). If the lines are perpendicular, the distance will measure exactly 5 feet. If it doesn't, the lines aren't perpendicular and you'll need to adjust the position of one of the lines.

2 **DIG FOOTINGS.** For a slab like this one, dig a 12- to 16-inch-deep trench around the perimeter for a 12-inch-wide footing (page 63). Then excavate at least 4 inches of soil from the interior and replace it with 4 inches of pea gravel for drainage. If the mason's lines are in your way, temporarily loosen them while you dig.

3 **BUILD FORMS.** Slab foundations use forms to define the sides of the slab. These are 2-by boards held in place with stakes. Before you pour the concrete, add rebar and wire mesh to help prevent it from cracking. Here, #5 rebar is placed on bricks in the bottom of the perimeter trench so the concrete will flow around it. A 6-mil vapor barrier will be laid over the gravel slab section and #10 reinforcing mesh on top of that, inset 2 inches from the forms. As with the rebar, bricks will raise the mesh so the concrete can flow around it.

4 **POUR CONCRETE.** Now you're ready to pour. For a slab foundation, the concrete truck will arrive with a load of concrete and the crew will quickly pour it into the form. Level the surface with the aid of a screed—typically a long, straight 2 by 4 or 2 by 6. Drag the screed with a sawing motion back and forth along the top of the form, then smooth the concrete with a bull float by dragging it carefully over the concrete (see inset at right).

5 **INSTALL ANCHORS.** With a slab foundation, the shed attaches to the slab via anchors set into the concrete. For maximum holding power, these are typically shaped like a J. On the slab, snap a chalk line to mark the center of the mudsills and then measure and mark anchor locations per your plans. Push each anchor into the wet concrete and wiggle it to get the concrete to fill in around it. Mist the slab with water and cover it with a layer of plastic. Keep the surface moist for two to three days.

FLOOR FRAMING

ONCE YOU'VE FINISHED A SLAB FOUNDATION, YOU'RE READY FOR THE WALLS; for wall-building details, see pages 70–73. However, if your plans call for a wood-framed floor, you'll need to build that first. Here's how.

The key to floor framing is to start with straight, parallel beams or rim joists atop temporary supports—like skids or piers—or permanent footings or foundation walls. Span the rim joists with floor joists placed every 16 or 24 inches on center; joist dimensions and spans are determined by local codes. The floor frame is covered with sheathing or subflooring (page 46), usually ³/₄-inch tongue-and-groove plywood or OSB (oriented strand board).

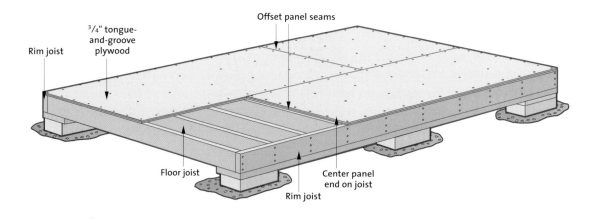

Offset panel seams

³/₄" tongue-and-groove plywood

Rim joist

Floor joist

Center panel end on joist

Rim joist

Cut It Straight

One of the best ways to ensure accuracy when framing floors, walls, or a roof is to make precise, straight cuts. For safety, support long pieces of lumber in two places on both sides of the cut. For shorter pieces, use sawhorses and allow space for cutoffs to fall away. For repeat cuts, make simple jigs to mark lumber quickly and accurately.

A speed square can help guide cuts with a circular saw, as shown at left. Place it on the workpiece so the lip catches the edge. Butt the saw up against the square with the blade on the waste side of the marked line. Hold the square firmly in place as you push the saw through the cut, keeping the saw base in constant contact with the square.

Building a Platform Floor

Though floor framing is straightforward—rim joists, evenly spaced floor joists, and a top layer of plywood or OSB—it should be installed as precisely as possible; any imperfections will make it difficult to square up the structure's walls and roof.

1 **INSTALL RIM JOISTS.** First, cut a pair of straight rim joists to sit atop the foundation. In this example, pressure-treated rim joists are nailed to 2 by 8 mudsills, which in turn bridge evenly spaced concrete blocks below. (For a closer look at this foundation, see page 64.) In some locales, you may be required to lock joists or sills in place with steel ground anchors.

2 **MARK JOIST LOCATIONS.** Lay out joist spacings 16 or 24 inches on center along the rim joists. If the final spacing is less than the others, fine. If it's slightly more, add an extra joist.

3 **INSTALL JOISTS.** Now cut floor joists to length. Position them between the rim joists (be sure they're not twisted), then fasten them flush with the tops of the rim joists. Use either 3-inch outdoor screws or 16d galvanized nails, driving them through each rim joist and into the joist ends. Alternately, install joists using galvanized joist hangers (page 47).

4 **ADD THE SUBFLOOR.** Lay a full sheet of ¾-inch tongue-and-groove plywood or OSB across the joists so it's flush with the edges; trim ends as necessary to center any seams on joists. Tack the panel in place with 2-inch deck screws or 8d nails (for firmer flooring, first apply a bead of construction adhesive to the joists), but don't screw or nail along the leading edge just yet. Start the next row as shown with a half-sheet to offset the seams, and finish adding plywood. Then go back and add fasteners every 8 inches around the perimeter and 12 inches elsewhere.

WALLS

AFTER THE FOUNDATION AND FLOOR ARE COMPLETE, you can start framing the walls, one of the most satisfying parts of building a shed or garage. A typical wall consists of vertical 2 by 4 wall studs spaced 16 or 24 inches on center. These stand between the bottom, or sole, plate (attached to the subfloor) and a top plate, which is later doubled when the walls are positioned. On slab foundations, the sole plate is called a mudsill and is usually pressure-treated wood.

Where an opening is made in the wall for a window or door, a horizontal framing member called a header is installed to assume the load of the wall studs that were removed. The makeup of a header varies according to the distance spanned and the load carried, but most are made from two 2-by members on edge with a $1/2$-inch plywood spacer between them—which adds up to $3^{1}/_{2}$ inches, the thickness of a 2 by 4 wall.

The header is supported by trimmer studs (also called jack studs) that are attached to the inside face of full-length studs known as king studs. The shorter pieces that run between the header and the top plate or from the underside of a rough sill to the sole plate or mudsill are called cripple studs.

In most cases, the rough opening for a window or door should be $1/2$ to $3/4$ inch wider and taller than the unit you're installing (consult the manufacturer's instruction sheet for the recommended gap). This extra space lets you adjust the unit for level and plumb.

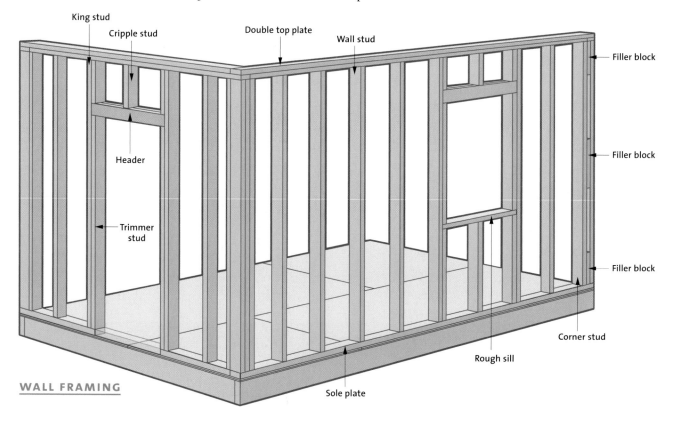

WALL FRAMING

Assembling a Wall

Before starting, double-check your plans for overall wall heights and confirm rough openings for windows and doors.

1 MARK THE PLATES. The best way to make sure that wall studs align is to mark their locations on the top and bottom plates for each wall at the same time. Make sure to choose lumber as straight as possible for these critical parts, and measure and cut them carefully. Align the plate ends and, if you prefer, screw them together temporarily. Set the plates on edge and, measuring from one end, make a mark at $1\frac{1}{2}$ inches and another at $15\frac{1}{4}$ inches (for 16-inch-on-center spacing) or $23\frac{1}{4}$ inches (for 24-inch-on-center spacing). Use a square and a pencil to continue these marks across both plates. Then measure and mark a line every 16 or 24 inches from these lines to indicate stud placement.

2 ATTACH WALL STUDS. Now separate the top and bottom plates. (On a slab foundation, position the mudsill on the slab and transfer the anchors' locations onto it; drill slightly oversize holes for the anchors to pass through.)

Then cut sufficient studs to length for the wall, and end-nail them as shown to the top and bottom plates with 16d nails, taking care to align the studs with the marks you made on the plates. For nailing tips, see the feature box below. *continued* ▶▶

Nailing It

The key to driving a big nail is to start with small hammer taps, then progress to looser, fuller swings.

Face-nailing is easy. Toenailing (left) is trickier; the aim here is to drive the nail at about a 30-degree angle. For beginners, it's sometimes easiest to drill a small pilot hole for the nail to follow. If you'd rather not toenail, try screws instead, or consider using metal framing connectors (page 47).

Some siding and trim jobs call for finish nails. To avoid ugly hammer dings, first drive the nail in until it's about $\frac{1}{8}$ inch above the wood, then tap its head below the surface with the hammer and a nailset (above).

3 **FRAME ROUGH OPENINGS.** If the wall section you're building includes windows or doors, you'll need to frame their rough openings. Cut and assemble headers as required. Also cut king, trimmer, and cripple studs and rough sills (if needed) per your plan.

Attach the king studs between the top and bottom plates and secure the trimmer studs to these. Place each header on top of the trimmers and fasten it to the trimmer and king studs. Complete the rough openings by installing cripple studs and sills as needed.

4 **RAISE THE WALL.** With a helper or two, lift the wall so its top plate is about waist high. Align the outside edge of the bottom plate with the outside edge of the floor or slab. Raise the wall upright by "walking" your hands down the studs. (On a slab foundation, make sure all the anchors pass through the mudsill.)

Add Siding Now?

For a small structure like a shed, wall sheathing and/or siding is sometimes more easily installed while the wall is flat on the ground. If this is your choice, be sure the wall is square first, then attach the siding as described on pages 80–83. The downside? You may need extra helpers when raising the walls—they're appreciably heavier with the siding attached.

5 **BRACE THE WALL.** Keep each wall upright until the remaining walls are in place by using a pair of 1 by 4 braces, one at each end. Nail the far end of each brace to a stake driven into the ground. To nail the near end, first use a level to adjust the wall section as needed to bring it into plumb. When everything is in position, have a helper nail or screw the brace to the wall section. After you've done this, take the time to double-check for plumb before moving on to the next wall. Quite often the act of securing the wall to the brace will shift it out of plumb; readjust as necessary.

6 **SECURE THE WALLS.** Also measure diagonals inside the structure and adjust for square; check the walls for level, and shim if needed.

Then attach each wall section to the slab or floor. For a slab foundation, place washers over the anchor bolts and thread on nuts. For wood floors, drive nails or screws every 16 inches or so through the sole plate and into the floor. The fasteners should penetrate about halfway into the floor joists or rim joists. Don't drive nails through the bottom plate in a doorway—this piece will be cut away when framing is done.

You'll need to add extra studs at the corners (see the drawing on page 70) so you can securely attach the wall sections to each other. Space these studs away from the end studs with filler blocks. Then start at one corner and nail together the walls with 16d nails. Repeat at the next corner. It's a good idea to check for level and plumb one more time, as the walls may have shifted slightly. Remove the temporary wood braces.

7 **DOUBLE THE TOP PLATE.** The tops of the walls are fixed together by adding another top plate (a "double" top plate). This second plate also creates a rigid structure that will help support the roof. Cut the double top plates to lengths that overlap the first top plates' joints. Secure the double top plates to the top plates with 8d nails every 16 inches or so. Drive in two nails at the ends of the plates that overlap intersecting walls. Use a handsaw or a reciprocating saw to remove the bottom plate in any door openings.

ROOFING

MOST SHED, GARAGE, AND BARN ROOFS ARE VARIATIONS ON THE SIMPLE GABLE ROOF, with evenly spaced rafters running from the top plates of two opposite walls up to the ridge board. A roof overhang often extends past the walls. The ends of the rafters are usually covered with trim called fascia.

Rafter size varies depending on the size of the structure, from 2 by 4s for a small shed to 2 by 10s or larger members for garages and barns. They're usually spaced on 16-inch or 24-inch centers. (Check with your building department for rafter dimensions and spacing required by local codes.) The ridge board is usually one size larger than the rafters (for example, a 2 by 8 ridge board for 2 by 6 rafters).

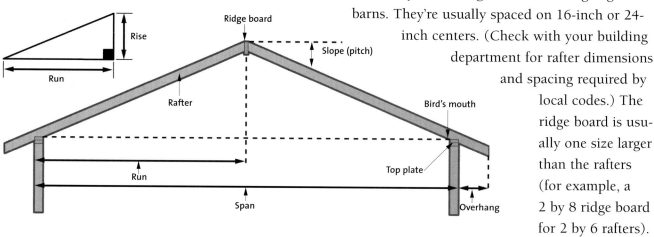

The slope, or pitch, of a roof is defined as a rafter's vertical rise in inches (or unit rise) per 12 inches of horizontal run. For example, a rafter that rises 5 inches for every 12 inches of run has a 5:12 or 5-in-12 slope. Roofs with steeper slopes require longer rafters and are better able to shed snow (use a minimum of 6 in 12 for snowy areas). Roofs with lower slopes work fine in warmer climates, though you'll generally want a slope of at least 3 in 12 for water runoff. (Asphalt shingles require a 4-in-12 or greater slope.)

Hip Framing

Because of the multiple angled cuts required for some of its rafters, a hip roof can be one of the more complicated options for roof framing. Adding to the confusion are the specialized names of many of the parts. Common rafters (blue in the drawing) run the full distance

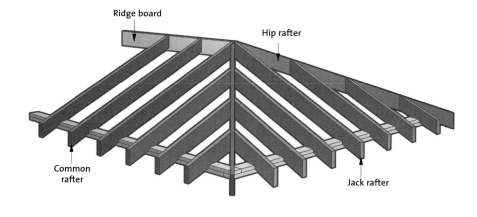

from the ridge board (shown as yellow) to the double top plates. Hip rafters (green) connect to the ridge at an angle where the two planes of the roof meet. Jack rafters (shown as red) run from the hip rafters to the plates.

Joists or No Joists?

Ceiling joists are horizontal framing members that span the top plates of the structure and prevent the roof load from blowing the walls apart. Small sheds won't require joists; larger sheds and garages might. As with rafters, the size of the joists depends on the size of the structure. As a general rule, the larger the structure, the larger the joists required. Typical joist spacing is 16 or 24 inches on center.

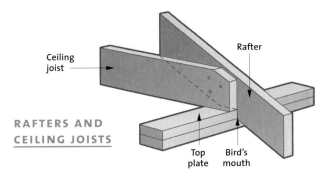

RAFTERS AND CEILING JOISTS

Eaves and Soffits

The area where the rafters meet the top plate is called the eave. When the rafters extend past the walls of a structure, they create an open area below the eave that's called a soffit. Typically, the rafter ends are covered with fascia. The soffit may be left open or closed in, as shown below.

The area where the roof meets the gable-end wall is sometimes called the rake. Some sheds have overhangs here, too, formed by ladder-like frames or blocking called outriggers. For an example, see the drawing on page 105.

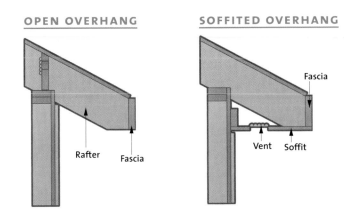

OPEN OVERHANG

SOFFITED OVERHANG

Trusses

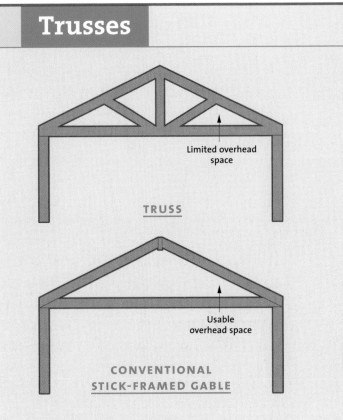

TRUSS

CONVENTIONAL STICK-FRAMED GABLE

As structures get larger, the framing members of conventional roofs must get beefier to handle the larger span. An alternative is to use prefabricated trusses designed to support a roof over a wide span. Well-designed trusses eliminate the need for load-bearing partitions below and greatly simplify framing so the roof can be put up quickly. However, one disadvantage to using roof trusses is the loss of attic space.

All trusses consist of three main parts: upper chords serving as rafters, lower chords acting as ceiling joists, and web members that tie the chords together. The parts are typically held together with metal or wood gusset plates. Different truss designs have different span potentials.

Engineered trusses can be ordered through most full-service lumberyards—just provide them with the building size and the desired roof pitch. You can also make and install your own trusses; for details, see the project on page 146.

Framing a Roof

Three cuts are needed to make the classic rafter: a plumb cut where the rafter meets the ridge board, a plumb cut at the eave end, and a bird's mouth to allow the rafter to fit onto the top plate of the wall. Expect some trial and error.

Depending on your shed plan, you may or may not need to add ceiling joists to span the walls. If you do, cut them to length and install them when framing the roof.

1 **MAKE A RAFTER TEMPLATE.** The most precise and efficient way to cut rafters is first to make a test rafter from a piece of rafter stock (for sheds, typically a 2 by 4 or 2 by 6). Consult your plans and carefully make the top and bottom plumb cuts and the bird's mouth (see facing page).

After you have made the test rafter, cut a second one. Using a helper, hold them temporarily in position with a scrap of 2-by material in between to serve as a ridge board and check the fit. If everything looks good, make your best rafter into a jig by tacking scraps of wood along one edge as shown; then use it to mark the remaining rafters quickly and accurately.

2 **MARK THE TOP PLATES.** Measure and mark the position of the rafters on the double top plates, making sure to start at the same end where you began measuring the wall studs; this ensures that rafters with the same spacings will be directly over the studs. Trim the ridge board to length and transfer the rafter layout from the double top plates to the ridge board.

3 **INSTALL RAFTERS.** End-nail the first rafter to the ridge board, then toenail the second rafter to the ridge board. Lift the assembly into place so the bird's mouth notches fit over the double top plates. Have a helper support the opposite end of the ridge board while you check to make sure that the ridge board is level and add a brace to keep it in place. Align the bottom of each rafter with the marks on the double top plate and attach with 16d nails. Add the rafters at the opposite end. Continue adding rafters until the roof framing is complete.

4 **ADD FASCIA.** Once the rafters are in place, you can add fascia. Fascia covers the ends of the rafters to protect them and provide a more finished look; a common fascia material is 1 by 6 preprimed pine. Depending on your shed plans, you may want to cover the gable-end rafters with fascia as well. Secure the fascia to each rafter end with 8d galvanized finish nails.

Cutting a Bird's Mouth

One way to scribe a bird's mouth is to have a helper hold the top end of a rafter against a scrap of ridge board that's temporarily supported with vertical braces while you hold its tail against the end of the top plate and draw around it to mark the notch in the rafter. Or you can mark the cuts with a framing square as shown at left. Position the framing square on the rafter so the blade and the tongue measurement marks align with the rafter edges to coincide with the rise and run of the roof.

Next, set the blade of a circular saw for maximum depth and make the bird's mouth cuts. Stop the cuts where the lines intersect. This won't cut out the notches completely, but cutting past the marks would weaken the rafter. Complete the cuts with a handsaw. If necessary, use a sharp chisel to clean up any rough edges, especially in the corners so the notches will rest flat on the top plates.

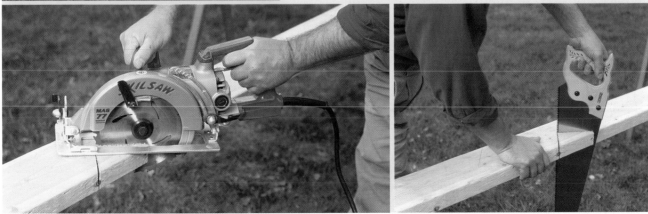

Adding Asphalt Shingles

Asphalt shingles are inexpensive and easy to apply, and they will last for years. (For details on roofing products, see pages 48–49.) But before you install them, you'll first need to install plywood sheathing. Even if code allows for thin sheathing, avoid anything less than ¹/₂ inch thick, as it won't provide as solid a nailing base as thicker sheathing offers.

The most critical part of installing shingles is the starter course. This course is placed with the tabs up instead of down to position the adhesive so it will help secure the first full row to the roof.

1 **INSTALL SHEATHING.** Apply plywood sheathing atop the roof framing, beginning at the bottom corner of one side. Place the long sides perpendicular to the rafters, trimming the sheets as necessary so the short ends are centered on rafters. Leave a ¹/₈-inch expansion gap between panels, and secure the panels to the rafters with 8d galvanized nails every 6 inches along the ends and every 12 inches elsewhere. Start the second row with a half-sheet to keep seams from aligning and weakening the roof. Add panels until the entire roof is sheathed.

2 **ROLL OUT ROOFING FELT.** Adding a layer of roofing felt (also called tar paper) on top of the sheathing and fascia protects the roofing from moisture. To align the first row of 36-inch-wide felt, snap a chalk line 35⁵/₈ inches above the eave (this provides a ³/₈-inch overhang). Then, allowing for a 2-inch overlap of each row, snap each successive line at 34 inches. Start applying strips from the bottom up, taking care to align their tops with the chalk lines. Where two strips meet at a vertical seam, overlap them at least 4 inches. Use only enough staples or nails to hold the felt in place until the shingles can be installed.

3 **ADD DRIP EDGE.** Before adding the asphalt shingles, protect the edges of the roof with drip edge. Drip edge is malleable aluminum that's preformed into a right angle with a slight lip along one edge to help direct water runoff away from the fascia and exterior siding. Cut a 45-degree miter at each end with metal snips. Press the drip edge in place so it butts firmly against the fascia, and secure it every 12 inches or so with roofing nails.

4 **INSTALL A STARTER COURSE.** Asphalt shingles use a self-sealing mastic to fuse the shingles together once they're heated by the sun. In order for the first full course of shingles to fasten to the front edge of the roof, a special starter row is installed. The starter row consists of 7-inch strips cut from full shingles and installed upside down (with the tab part cut off) along the eaves to position the mastic near the edge, where it will stick to the first full row installed. Because all the shingles will use the starter row as a reference, it's important to make sure it goes down straight. Start by snapping a chalk line on the felt to define the top of the starter course. Secure the starter row with roofing nails 3 inches above the eaves.

5 **ADD STANDARD COURSES.** The first and remaining courses are all installed with the tabs pointing down. Install the first course of shingles on top of the starter row, allowing a ½-inch overhang. Nail each shingle to the roof just above the slot between the tabs. Snap a chalk line 10 inches up from the bottom of the first course, and install the second course, offsetting it horizontally by a half-tab. Continue snapping reference lines and adding courses until you reach the ridge.

To save time, let the shingles overhang the gable ends. Then come back once the side of the roof is complete and trim them all at once. You can do this with a sharp utility knife or a pair of heavy-duty shears.

6 **ATTACH THE RIDGE CAP.** At the ridge, use ready-made ridge shingles or cut your own 12-inch squares from standard shingles. On the most visible side of the shed, snap a line that's parallel to and 6 inches down from the ridge. Starting at the end opposite the prevailing wind, apply the shingles, leaving a 5-inch exposure; align the edges with the chalk marks. Nail on each side, 5½ inches from the butt and 1 inch from the outside edge.

SIDING

TO SEAL UP YOUR SHED OR GARAGE, siding is every bit as important as a good roof. The color, texture, and pattern you choose will also affect your structure's style, so you will want to pick a material that both looks good and wears well. For options, see pages 50–51.

Sheathing (page 46) is used under some siding materials for a variety of purposes: to help brace the structure, to serve as a solid base for nailing, and to improve insulation. Check your local building code to determine whether structural sheathing is required for the type of siding you've chosen.

Sheathing can be installed horizontally or vertically. Vertical sheathing works best for 8-foot-tall walls because it can be nailed along all four edges. Position each sheet so the edges are centered on the studs. Nail sheets to the studs with 8d nails every 6 inches along the edge and every 12 inches elsewhere. Leave a $\frac{1}{8}$-inch expansion gap between panels. It's often easiest to apply sheathing right over openings for windows and doors, then cut them out later.

Once you've installed the sheathing, some local codes require you to add a layer of either building paper or house wrap, as shown above. This moisture barrier gives your shed an extra layer of defense against wind and weather.

PLYWOOD SIDING

Trim overhang at corner

Sheathing

Building paper

Center edge over stud

Clean Cuts in Sheet Products

The key to making clean, straight cuts in plywood and other sheet materials is to clamp a straightedge to the sheet for your saw to follow. If you're using a circular saw, measure the distance from the edge of the saw's baseplate to the blade, and clamp the straightedge at this distance from the cutting line. Be sure to support the sheet on sawhorses.

When you're using a circular saw or jigsaw, cut the sheets on the back side to avoid splintering the face, since these saws cut on the upstroke. The sheets will be flipped over when installed, though, so be extra careful when determining the cutting lines.

Finally comes the part that shows: the siding. Plywood siding goes up quickly and often does double duty as sheathing. For instructions on how to install traditional solid-board siding, see pages 82–83. Two other commonly used options—fiber-cement and plywood lap boards—are installed in a similar manner.

Windows and doors with external flanges or brick molding are normally installed after sheathing is on but before siding is attached. Units without flanges can be added after the siding is on.

Installing Sheet Siding

Plywood siding applied directly to studs without sheathing must be at least $^3/_8$ inch thick for studs on 16-inch centers, and at least $^1/_2$ inch thick for studs on 24-inch centers. Panels as thin as $^5/_{16}$ inch may be applied over sheathing.

Plywood may be mounted either vertically or horizontally. Vertical installation is the most common method, since it minimizes the number of horizontal joints. If you choose a horizontal pattern, stagger vertical end joints and nail the long, horizontal edges into fire blocks (2 by 4 blocks nailed between the studs) or other nailing supports to make sure the joints are protected.

1 **INSTALL THE FIRST SHEET.** Start by aligning the first sheet vertically at one corner so its edge is flush with the corner framing. Check that the opposite edge reaches the center of a wall stud, and make sure the edge is plumb; shift the panel and trim as necessary. Attach the siding to the studs using 8d galvanized nails every 6 inches around the perimeter and every 12 inches elsewhere.

2 **ADD REMAINING SHEETS.** Install remaining sheets, leaving a $^1/_8$-inch expansion gap between them. Some panels have shiplap edges; nail them as shown below. If your plywood doesn't have these edges, simply butt and caulk the joints or cover them with vertical battens.

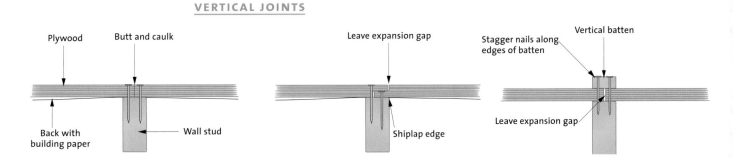

VERTICAL JOINTS

Plywood | Butt and caulk

Back with building paper | Wall stud

Leave expansion gap | Shiplap edge

Stagger nails along edges of batten | Vertical batten | Leave expansion gap

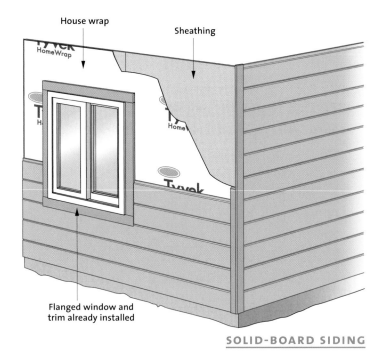

House wrap

Sheathing

Flanged window and
trim already installed

SOLID-BOARD SIDING

Applying Solid-board Siding

While many board sidings seem similar, for proper installation you must treat each pattern individually. Some board siding requires sheathing; for others, it's optional. With beveled or clapboard siding, windows and doors are usually installed first, then trim and casings are added; the siding boards butt into these to eliminate ugly gaps where siding meets trim. Flatter siding shapes can be applied first, then trim added on top. Some patterns may be installed either vertically or horizontally; while others must be installed horizontally. What's the rule here? Be sure to ask your supplier and/or building inspector what's best for your chosen product.

Before you begin nailing up siding boards, figure out how you want to treat the corners (see facing page). When planning your layout, try to align board rows with windows, doors, and other openings; with horizontal siding, a slight adjustment to the baseline may do it. If you must butt board ends, stagger these joints as much as possible between successive rows.

1 **ATTACH VAPOR BARRIER.** First add house wrap or building paper to limit air movement through walls and prevent heat loss and damage due to moisture. Minimize seams; when they are necessary, provide at least a 12-inch overlap. Leave excess around window and door openings so you can wrap it around the opening to create a seal. For details, see page 86.

2 **START NAILING ON SIDING.** Here, we're working with horizontal clapboard siding. First, nail on any inside and outside corner boards, plus any window and door casings required (page 87). Then snap a level line for the top of the base course and nail a small starter strip (see below) along the bottom edge of the sheathing to give the siding the proper pitch.

Align the base course with the chalk line, and nail it in place. Overlap the next piece and repeat up the wall. Check the siding periodically for level; if things are getting off, adjust the following courses gradually to bring things back in line—your eye won't notice small changes.

THREE CORNER DETAILS

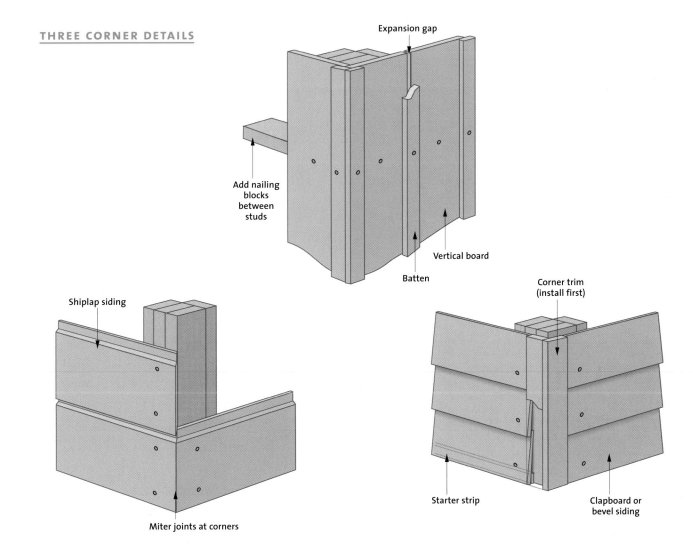

Expansion gap

Add nailing blocks between studs

Vertical board

Batten

Shiplap siding

Miter joints at corners

Corner trim (install first)

Starter strip

Clapboard or bevel siding

WINDOWS AND DOORS

IF YOU'VE SIZED THE ROUGH OPENING PROP-ERLY (page 70), installing a manufactured window or door is straightforward. Essentially, the job consists of centering the door or window frame in the opening, shimming it level and plumb, and securing it to the framing.

Flanged windows and doors are normally installed after any sheathing is on but before siding is attached. Windows and doors with attached casings, or brickmold, are typically installed before bevel siding but after flat siding like plywood. Units without flanges or casings can be added once the siding is on. Confused? Ask your supplier for the best approach with your chosen products.

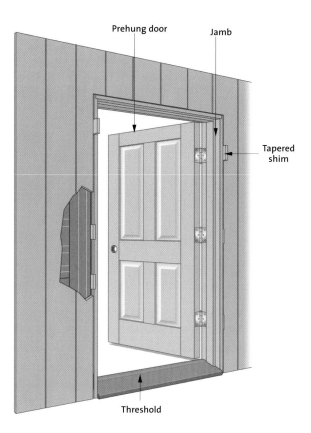

Prehung door   Jamb

Tapered shim

Threshold

DOOR ANATOMY

Build Your Own Door

Several projects in Chapter Four call for doors you make yourself. Although you could choose traditional doormakers' joints like mortise and tenon or tongue and groove, the simplest way to build shed doors is in layers: the outside boards (which often match the surrounding siding) and an added support frame.

The Z-frame shown here is a good choice for joining vertical boards. First lay out the boards face-up as shown above and pick the order you like. Then

flip the boards face down, snug them together, and lay out the brac-ing as shown at left. Secure the braces with nails or screws (we used stainless steel outdoor screws) that are slightly shorter than the combined thickness of the parts (otherwise, they'll poke through!). If you like, first add a bead of exterior glue to the backs of the braces.

Installing a Prehung Door

Installing a door the traditional way means constructing a door frame, attaching it to the rough opening, hinging the door to the frame, and installing a latch or lockset. If you buy a prehung door, much of the work has been done for you: the jambs are assembled and the door is hinged to the jamb. On exterior prehung doors, the threshold is typically in place. The only tricky parts are making sure the unit is level and plumb and that the frame doesn't bow or twist as you install it. Check and recheck before securing the unit to the framing.

① POSITION THE DOOR. Slide the prehung unit into the rough opening and center it all around. If you plan to add an interior finish floor later, raise the doorjambs to this height above the subfloor with scrap blocks.

SHIM STRATEGY

Fine-tune the fit of a door or window within an over-size rough opening using pairs of tapered wood shims. Tap in one from one side and the other from the opposite side until they are just snug against the jambs; then nail through the jambs and both shims into the framing. Score thin shims with a utility knife and snap them off flush with the jambs. Trim thicker ones with a reciprocating saw or a handsaw.

② SHIM IT PLUMB AND LEVEL. Insert pairs of tapered shims around the perimeter, snugging them between the jambs and the trimmer studs or header. Adjust the shims as necessary to make the unit plumb and level.

③ NAIL DOOR TO FRAMING. To secure the frame, drive galvanized finish nails through the interior jambs and shims and into the trimmer studs and header. Trim off any protruding shims. Also secure doors with nailing flanges or pre-installed brickmold from outside, as shown at left.

Installing a Window

In general, wooden windows are attached to the sheathing by nailing through the exterior casing, or brickmold, on the outside. For aluminum, clad, or vinyl windows, drive nails or screws through the factory-installed nailing flanges on the outside perimeter of the window. If your window has neither casing nor flanges, secure it through the interior jambs and into the trimmer studs, header, and rough sill surrounding the opening. Exact installation methods vary, so always follow the manufacturer's recommendations.

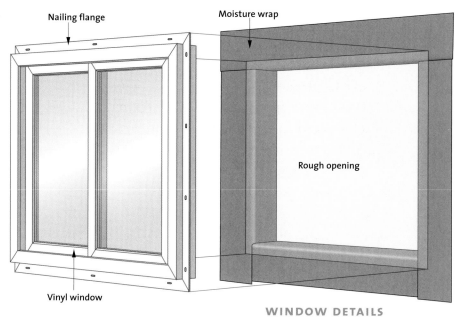

Nailing flange

Moisture wrap

Rough opening

Vinyl window

WINDOW DETAILS

1 **CUT OUT THE OPENING.** If you've already applied plywood sheathing or siding, you'll need to remove it from the rough opening. From inside the structure, drill ¾-inch access holes through the sheathing at the corners of the rough opening. Use a reciprocating saw (shown) or jigsaw to cut the opening.

2 **APPLY MOISTURE BARRIER.** If you're adding house wrap or building paper, you should have left enough excess around the window and door openings so that you can wrap it into the framed opening to create a seal. Alternatively, use self-adhesive moisture wrap that sticks to the sheathing and overlaps the opening.

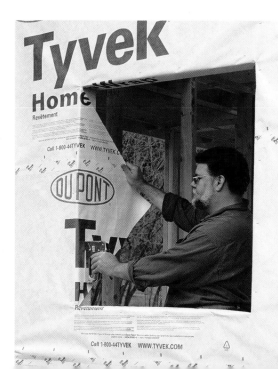

3 **INSTALL THE WINDOW.** Before you place the window in the opening, run a bead of exterior-grade caulk around the perimeter to ensure a tight seal. With the aid of a helper, if required, lift the unit into the opening. Have your helper hold the unit while you go inside to adjust its position.

From inside, raise the window to the correct height above the rough sill with shims or wood blocks. Check the top of the unit with a carpenter's level. If it's not level, adjust the shims.

Then slip pairs of tapered shims between the jamb and the framed opening, following manufacturer's instructions. (See the tip on page 85.) Check for level and plumb, and adjust the shims as necessary. For windows with attached exterior trim or brickmold, drive galvanized finish nails through the trim and into the framing. With nailing flanges, use either headed nails or screws. For windows without trim or flanges, drive finish nails through the jambs at the shim locations and into the framing.

Finishing Off with Trim

All that's left to complete your shed's exterior is to install trim around windows and doors, and along the top and/or bottom of the exterior walls if desired. Trim can be minimal or fanciful; joints can be either butted (as shown here) or mitered.

For exterior trim, 1 by 4 redwood or cedar is tops but pricey; pine also works well. Preprimed trim is available that makes painting your trim a quick and easy task; otherwise, it's best to prime the backs of the boards before applying them.

A power miter saw (page 43) makes quick, clean, and accurate cuts; if you don't have one on hand, use a circular saw or a fine-toothed handsaw.

1 **APPLY TRIM.** Be sure to use galvanized finish nails that are long enough to penetrate through the siding and sheathing, then into the rough framing below. Stop hammering when the nail heads are about $1/8$ inch above the wood; drive them home with a nailset (page 71).

2 **SEAL THE JOINTS.** Complete your window or door trim by running a bead of silicone caulk around the exterior trim to create a water-tight seal.

FINISHING TOUCHES

ONCE THERE'S A ROOF ON YOUR STRUCTURE AND THE EXTERIOR IS CLOSED IN, you can turn to any finish work. This might include adding electrical circuits, plumbing, or insulation and covering the interior walls. You may also want to build an exterior access ramp or stairs.

Adding Power

Any shed, garage, or barn you build will be more functional and flexible if you run power to it. You'll be able to light up the interior at night, use power tools and appliances—even install heating and cooling. Getting the power there is the tough part; adding interior wiring is simpler. For details, see the Sunset book *Complete Home Wiring.*

Though you could run overhead wires to your shed, it's far better to run power underground (marked red, below) from your home's service panel. First make sure you have sufficient capacity available at the service panel. If in doubt, check with a licensed electrician. You may need to upgrade the panel—a potentially pricey proposition. With the power source established, you can either dig a trench (check local codes for the required depth) and bury UF (underground feeder) cable or encase separate wires in metal or plastic conduit.

Depending on your power needs, you may run a single 20-amp circuit that ends in a junction box, a 40- to 60-amp cable feeding a subpanel, or up to a 100-amp line that powers a new service panel. From this source, the wiring branches out into circuits—a single branch for an overhead light and a couple of receptacles, or

OUTBUILDING ELECTRICAL SYSTEM

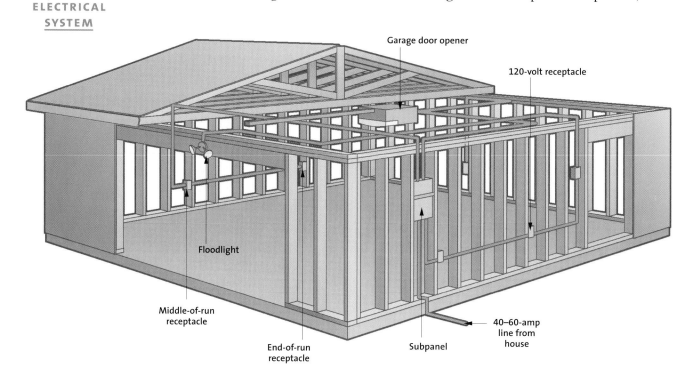

Garage door opener

120-volt receptacle

Floodlight

Middle-of-run receptacle

End-of-run receptacle

Subpanel

40–60-amp line from house

multiple branches. Nonmetallic (NM) cable makes interior wiring simple, since no conduit is required. Essentially, all you do is route the cable through ceilings and walls through access holes in studs or joists.

Check with your local building department. Electrical codes specify everything from how high a receptacle is mounted to the number of wires in a junction box.

Making final connections to a subpanel or service panel is best done by a licensed electrician. Make sure to have the wiring inspected before adding any wall coverings.

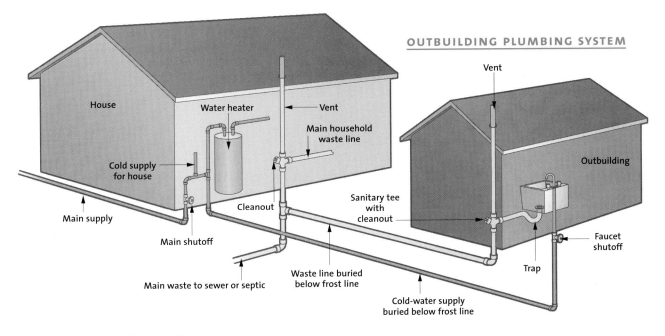

OUTBUILDING PLUMBING SYSTEM

House • Water heater • Vent • Main household waste line • Cold supply for house • Main supply • Main shutoff • Cleanout • Sanitary tee with cleanout • Main waste to sewer or septic • Waste line buried below frost line • Cold-water supply buried below frost line • Vent • Outbuilding • Faucet shutoff • Trap

Running Plumbing

Convenient as it is to have running water in a shed, garage, or barn, it may not be feasible. A small budget might rule it out, and your local climate may also limit your options.

In warm climates, you might get by with burying a garden hose a few inches below the lawn, then making a simple drain pit to serve as the septic or sewer. In colder climates, though, water and waste lines must be installed well below the frost line—in some areas as much as 4 to 5 feet deep. Pipe depth, materials, and even who can make the connections will be defined by local code.

In a typical outbuilding, a single cold-water line is run from the house. Likewise, a waste line runs out to the building, but it slopes back toward the house so it will drain into the existing system.

At the new structure, the waste line terminates in a sanitary tee with a cleanout port. A vent pipe connects to the top of the sanitary tee and continues up through the roof. Another drainpipe connects to the sink via a trap. Here again, the piping must slope down toward the tee to allow drainage. A shutoff valve on the water supply line controls water flow to the sink faucet. If you want hot water, don't try to run an insulated line—install a water heater in the outbuilding instead.

Adding Insulation

Interior walls can be left bare or covered. Finishing off an interior wall or ceiling usually begins by installing insulation. Then the wall and/or ceiling coverings are attached to the framing.

Wall coverings around windows and doors should butt closely against the window or door jamb. Fill any gaps with insulating foam or scraps of fiberglass to prevent drafts. To add trim around these openings, see pages 92–93.

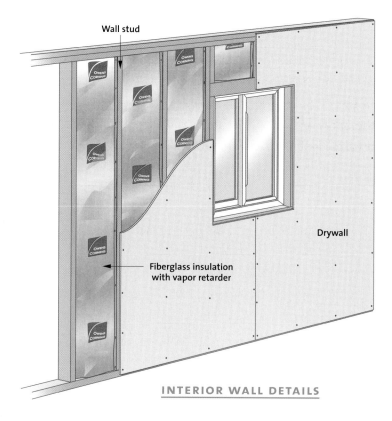

Wall stud

Drywall

Fiberglass insulation with vapor retarder

INTERIOR WALL DETAILS

INSTALLING FIBERGLASS. Measure from top to bottom, add 3 inches, and cut a strip of insulation to length with scissors or a utility knife. Be sure to wear gloves and a dust mask. Press the strip between the framing and overlap the facing onto the framing. Begin stapling at the top and work your way down both sides.

INSTALLING RIGID FOAM. Precut strips of rigid foam make installation a snap. Measure between top and bottom and cut the strip to match with a utility knife or a handsaw. For walls, it's best to apply a bead of construction adhesive around the perimeter of the foam to hold it until the wall covering is installed. On ceilings, first apply a generous bead of construction adhesive around the perimeter and an X from top to bottom, then press the strip into place.

Installing Drywall

Drywall, or gypsum wallboard, is popular for covering both walls and ceilings. Position the first sheet of drywall tight in a corner so the opposite edge is centered on a framing member. Wall sheets may be installed either vertically or horizontally. If the opposite edge of the sheet isn't centered on the studs, remove and trim it, as shown in the feature box below.

1 SECURE SHEETS TO FRAMING. Drywall nails go in quickly, but they have a tendency to "pop" over time as the studs dry out. Drywall screws are stronger. If you're using screws, drive them in so they sit just below the surface, but don't break the paper covering.

2 APPLY TAPE. To conceal the joints between sheets, apply drywall tape over the gaps. Tape may be self-adhesive or nonstick. With self-adhesive tape, just press it into place. To apply nonstick tape, first spread on a thin amount of joint compound, then gently press the tape into the compound with a wide-blade putty knife.

3 ADD JOINT COMPOUND. Apply a first full coat of joint compound over both the tape and the "dimples" left by the screws, using a 4- to 6-inch-wide drywall knife. Spread the compound as smoothly as possible—don't depend on sanding to remove anything but minor imperfections.

4 FEATHER AND SMOOTH. When the first coat has dried (after about 24 hours), apply a second coat with a wider drywall knife. Work the compound gently away from the joint to "feather" it for a smooth transition. Give the still-wet walls a very light sanding with handheld sandpaper or a pole sander (a tool with a sanding pad attached to a pole) to knock off imperfections. When the joint compound is dry, smooth the surface to remove any remaining imperfections. Use a slightly damp drywall sponge and rub with a swirling motion to level the surface.

Cutting Drywall

To trim drywall to size, draw a line with a straight-edge (a drywall T-square is ideal) and cut along the line with a sharp utility knife. Flip the sheet over and bend back one end to snap the sheet. Run your utility knife along the inside crease to cut completely through the sheet. If necessary, smooth the cut edge with a rasp or file—a perforated rasp works great.

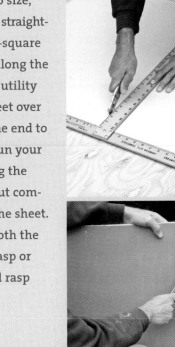

Installing Interior Window and Door Trim

Install interior window and door trim after wall coverings are in place. Typically, trim consists of two side casings and a head casing. Window trim may also include an apron and a finish sill. All these components are shown in the drawing at right. Some windows—especially flanged vinyl models—won't fill the entire depth of the opening, leaving some rough framing exposed. To trim out this gap, you'll need to add manufactured "extension jambs" or other strips of wood, as shown at right.

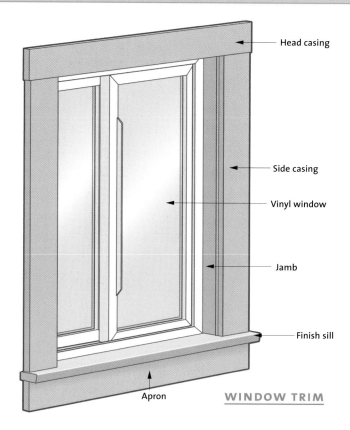

Head casing

Side casing

Vinyl window

Jamb

Finish sill

Apron

WINDOW TRIM

1 **INSULATE AROUND THE OPENING.** If you are insulating your building, take the time before you attach the interior trim to stuff some extra fiberglass insulation in any gaps between the window or door jamb and the framing. This will help reduce drafts and heat loss.

2 **MARK THE REVEAL.** Draw a setback line, or "reveal," about $1/4$ inch in from the inside edges of the window or door jamb. Align each of the side casings with this line and mark them where they intersect the top reveal line.

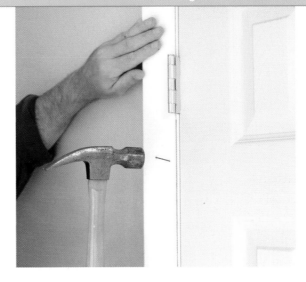

3 **ADD THE SIDE TRIM.** Cut the head and side casings to length with a power miter saw or a handsaw and a miter box. You can use either 45-degree miter joints, as shown in step 4, or butt joints (see drawing on facing page). Tack the side casings in place with 2-inch finish nails, aligning the inside edges with the reveal lines.

4 **INSTALL TOP TRIM.** Now tack the head casing in place, and if everything lines up, drive the nails home. Whenever you attach trim with nails, stop hammering when the head of the nail is about $\frac{1}{8}$ inch away from the surface. Drive the protruding nail the rest of the way in using a nailset (page 71). Set the nails about $\frac{1}{16}$ inch below the surface, fill with putty, and sand flush when dry.

If there are gaps between the interior trim and the wall covering, run a bead of paintable latex caulk around the trim to fill them. Smooth the joints with a putty knife.

Finish Sill?

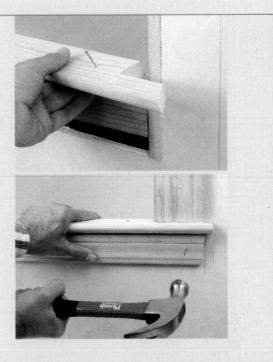

If you like the look of an interior finish sill (also called a stool) below your window, install it before adding the other trim. The trick is to notch the sill around the window jamb and wall covering as shown at right. Cut the notches with a jigsaw (page 43) or a handsaw. Normally the sill extends slightly past the outside edges of the side casings once installed. Nail the finish sill to the rough sill below.

With the sill in place, cut and attach side and head casings; note that even if your top casing joints are mitered, the bottoms of the side casings will be squared off where they met the sill.

Finally, cut and attach the apron, as shown at right. Typically, the apron lines up with the outside edges of the side casings, allowing the sill to extend beyond it. Nail the apron to the wall framing; then predrill and drive a few more finish nails through the sill into the edge of the apron.

Adding Stairs or Ramps

Stairs or a ramp must attach securely to your shed, garage, or barn with joist hangers or a ledger, and to a concrete or packed-gravel footing at ground level. Most building codes allow for a shallow footing installed over pea gravel for drainage; check with your local building department to be sure. When you chat with the building department folks, ask whether handrails are required for your stairs or ramp.

Stairs. Typical shed stairs consist of two or three stringers and treads (see the drawing below). To make your own, first establish the rise and run of the steps. Total rise is the distance from the ground to the floor of the structure; unit rise is the height of each step. Total run (how far the steps will extend out) requires a little math.

Start by dividing the total rise by 7 inches (the recommended rise or height of each step) to find out how many steps you'll need; round off to the nearest whole number. Then to find total run, multiply the unit run (or tread depth) you'd like by the number of treads—which is always one less than the number of steps. For safety, it's best for treads to be at least 10 inches deep. For example, a total rise of 40 inches divided by 7 inches equals 5.7; rounding up yields 6 steps (5 treads). So the total run in this case would be at least 5 times 10 inches, or 50 inches. To find your actual unit rise, divide your measured total rise by the number of steps. In this example, actual unit rise equals 40 inches divided by 6—roughly $6\frac{5}{8}$ inches.

STAIRS

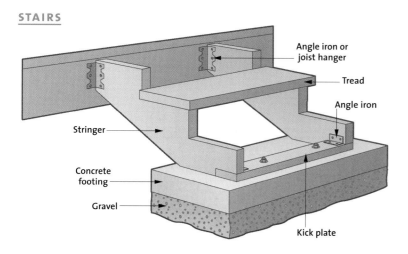

Angle iron or joist hanger

Tread

Angle iron

Stringer

Concrete footing

Gravel

Kick plate

Ramp. A ramp is easier to build than stairs because no treads are involved. All you need to do is decide on the slope of the ramp and cut the ends of the stringers accordingly. The slope is measured in inches of vertical rise per linear foot. A 1-in-8 slope will do for most utility work; for wheelchair access, use a 1-in-12 slope.

RAMP

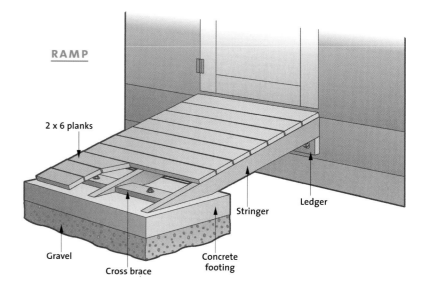

2 x 6 planks

Ledger

Stringer

Gravel

Cross brace

Concrete footing

PLATFORM STEPS

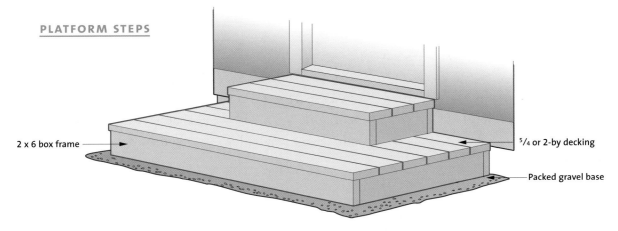

2 x 6 box frame

⁵/₄ or 2-by decking

Packed gravel base

Building Platform Steps

Want a simpler alternative to stairs? If your rise is modest, consider a set of platform steps, as shown above. These steps are basically a stack of interconnecting boxes built atop a firm footing. Each box is a simple wood frame (2 by 6s work well) topped with additional lumber. For a safe, comfortable stride, each box should be no more than 7 inches tall, but they may be as wide and deep as you like.

1 **BUILD THE FRAMES.** First, cut front and back frame pieces to length for each step, then ends and internal dividers (space these no more than 16 inches apart). Screw or nail the pieces together.

2 **ADD TREADS.** Top each platform with ⁵/₄ or 2-by treads; here we used ⁵/₄ by 6 composite decking. Our steps were sized so that the treads are flush in back but overlap the frame about an inch in front and on each side. Use deck screws to secure treads to the front, back, and internal dividers of each frame. For a tidier look, recess—or countersink—the screws below the surface.

3 **SECURE THE PLATFORMS.** Secure each frame to the one below it with screws or nails driven through the frames at an angle, as shown. Or, if you'd rather hide these fasteners, make connections on the insides of the frames before adding the top treads. Finally, secure the platform to the shed's siding or floor framing with additional fasteners.

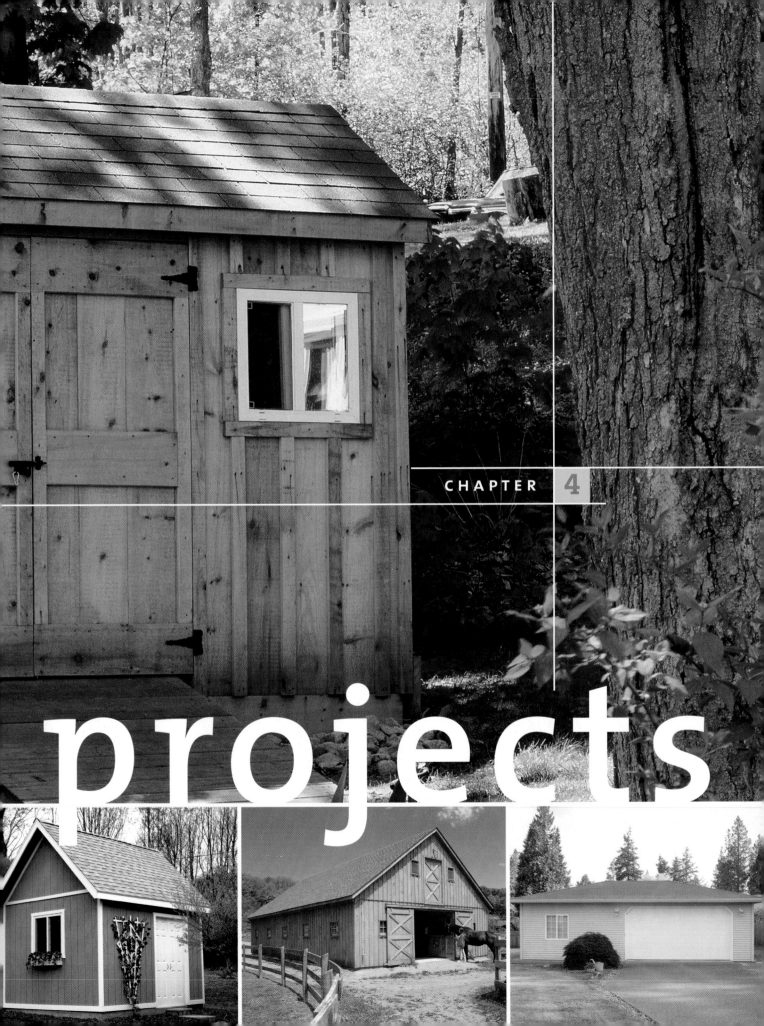

projects

LEAN-TO SHED

WHEN YOU JUST WANT COVERED SPACE, PLAIN AND SIM-PLE, LOOK TO THE LEAN-TO. This shed shares a wall with an adjacent structure to offer protection from the elements for firewood, outdoor furniture, garden tools, or toys. Build it in a weekend and put it to work right away. (To purchase plans for this shed, see page 159.)

DESIGN: GARLINGHOUSE COMPANY

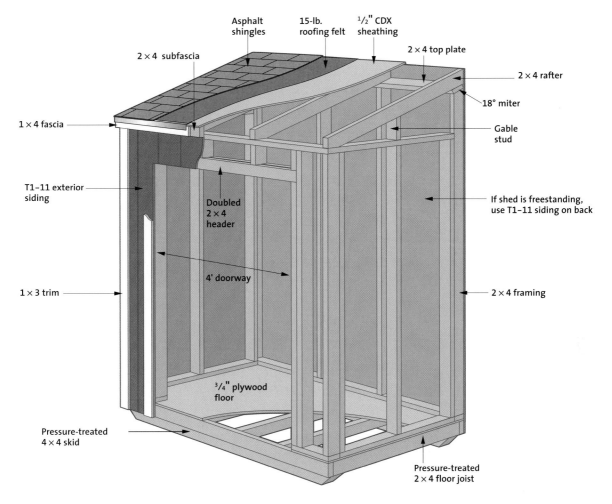

Asphalt shingles

15-lb. roofing felt

½" CDX sheathing

2 × 4 subfascia

2 × 4 top plate

2 × 4 rafter

18° miter

1 × 4 fascia

Gable stud

T1–11 exterior siding

If shed is freestanding, use T1–11 siding on back

Doubled 2 × 4 header

4' doorway

1 × 3 trim

2 × 4 framing

¾" plywood floor

Pressure-treated 4 × 4 skid

Pressure-treated 2 × 4 floor joist

Design Details

The lean-to shown here is 4 feet deep by 6 feet wide, but it's easy to expand to 8 feet in width by adding another stud to the back wall and shifting the door studs to 24 inches from the ends. The floor frame and roofing would also have to be expanded. And if it suits your fancy, place the door in one of the side walls.

While most sheds with lean-to roofs live up to their name by "leaning" into another structure, they can also be freestanding. If that's your wish, consider using concrete piers or poured footings and plan to sheath the back wall with exterior-rated T1-11 siding like the rest of the walls.

Materials List

• Pressure-treated skids	4 × 4
• Pressure-treated floor joists	2 × 4
• Exterior-grade plywood flooring	¾"
• Top plates, bottom plates, studs, header, trimmer studs, cripple studs, rafters, subfascia	2 × 4
• T1-11 exterior siding	⅝"
• CDX roof sheathing	½"
• Fascia	1 × 4
• Corner and door trim	1 × 3
• Drip edge and 15-lb. roofing felt	
• Asphalt shingles	
• Galvanized nails	
• Door hinges and latch	
• Paint or stain	

How to Build the Lean-to Shed

The floor frame for this small shed rests on pressure-treated skids (page 62) instead of a fixed foundation. If your site is sloped or has poor drainage, first excavate soil to a depth of 4 inches and replace it with gravel, then place your skids and floor atop that. Next, frame the walls and roof on top of the level platform and enclose them with plywood siding and asphalt shingles. Finally, build and hang a simple door and tidy things up with a little trim.

1 **FRAME THE FLOOR.** Cut two pressure-treated 4 by 4s to 6 feet long for skids. Do the same with two pressure-treated 2 by 4s for the rim joists. Cut six floor joists to 45 inches long and position them between the rim joists, 16 inches on center, as shown below; secure with 16d nails. Place the frame on the skids, shim it level as required, square it up, and toenail the floor joists to the skids. Cover the frame with ³/₄-inch exterior plywood.

2 **BUILD THE WALLS.** For the back wall, cut 6-foot-long top and bottom plates and lay out studs 24 inches on center. The wall studs are 8 feet long, with their top ends angled at 18 degrees. Build the back wall and nail it to the floor frame, bracing as necessary (page 73).

For the front wall, cut the top plate 6 feet long and two bottom plates each 1 foot long. Mark a 4-foot-wide door opening and the stud positions.

Cut four wall studs to 81¼ inches long, plus two 71½-inch-long trimmer studs. Also cut two 51-inch-long 2 by 4s, plus a same-size strip of ¹/₂-inch-thick plywood as a spacer (page 70), and nail them all together for a header. Assemble the wall and attach the header, then add four cripple studs on top as shown on the facing page. Secure the front wall to the floor and brace as needed.

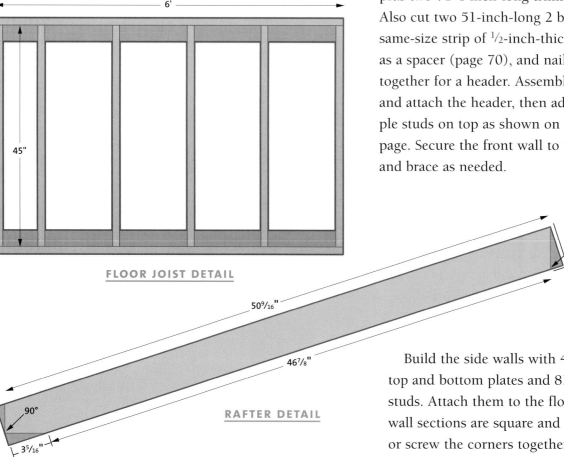

FLOOR JOIST DETAIL

6'

4'

45"

RAFTER DETAIL

50⁹/₁₆"

46⁷/₈"

72°

90°

3⁵/₁₆"

Build the side walls with 41-inch-long top and bottom plates and 81¼-inch-long studs. Attach them to the floor. When the wall sections are square and plumb, nail or screw the corners together.

3 **FRAME THE ROOF.** The roof framing consists of 2 by 4 rafters that rest on the front and back top plates. Cut four rafters as shown on the facing page. Toenail them to the top plates every 24 inches. Then cut a 2 by 4 gable stud to fit between the end rafter and the top plate of each side wall. Cut the 2 by 4 subfascia to length and attach it to the front ends of the rafters.

4 **ENCLOSE THE WALLS.** Next cut pieces of T1-11 siding to cover the front and the sides; save the cutouts to make the doors. Position the siding flush with the bottom of the rim joists and attach it with 8d galvanized nails every 8 inches or so.

5 **INSTALL THE ROOF.** Use $\frac{1}{2}$-inch CDX plywood to sheath the rafters, using 6d nails. Cut the side (or rake) trim to cover the exposed edges of the roof sheathing, and attach. Also cut and install the front fascia, aligning its bottom edge with the bottoms of the side rakes. Install drip edge and 15-pound roofing felt, and apply the shingles. (For more on roofing techniques, see pages 78–79.)

6 **ADD DOORS AND TRIM** Using leftover siding scraps, build a pair of doors to fit the opening, trimming them out with 1 by 3s (see door detail at right). Cut and install 1 by 3 trim along the shed's front corners and back edges, then around the top and both sides of the door opening. Prop the doors in the opening with wood shims or blocks and check the fit; they should be snug on the sides and have about $\frac{1}{2}$ inch of clearance top and bottom. Finally, attach the doors with strap hinges and add a door latch.

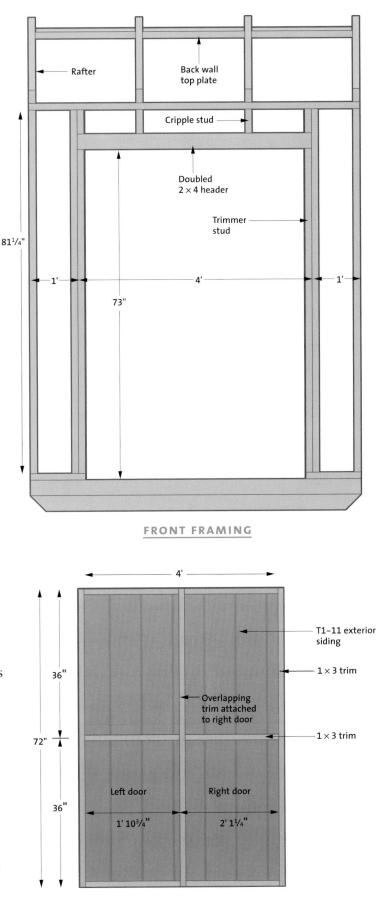

FRONT FRAMING

DOOR DETAIL

D E S I G N E R ' S   S K E T C H B O O K

Under-eave Storage Locker

Attached to the outside of the house, this 15½-inch-deep lean-to opens to reveal a surprisingly spacious storage area. The 72- by 80-inch opening accommodates two barn doors, which were built from rough-sawn fence lumber, but you could save time by purchasing exterior or screen doors. Adjust the size of your shed's opening to fit the doors you select.

You'll need one sheet of plywood to make the two ends and the floor module. (The designer used rough-sawn exterior plywood.) The exposed wood—pressure-treated rafters, filler blocks, front posts, and front beam—are Douglas fir, but you could opt for other woods.

Plan to preassemble the shed in manageable pieces—side walls, rafters, ledger, and floor; then paint if you wish, bring to the site, and install. Seal doors with stain or clear water sealer, then hang them with strap hinges, adding a handle and a hasp.

DESIGN: PETER O. WHITELEY

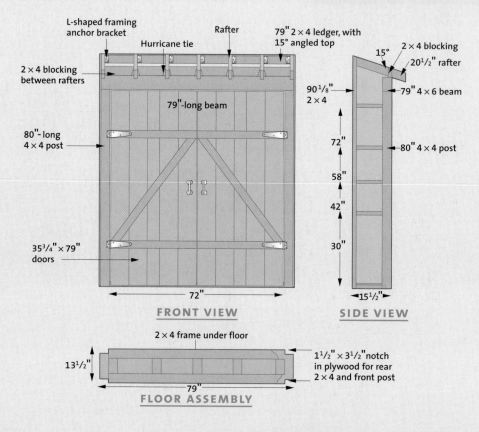

FRONT VIEW

- L-shaped framing anchor bracket
- Rafter
- 79" 2 × 4 ledger, with 15° angled top
- Hurricane tie
- 2 × 4 blocking between rafters
- 79"-long beam
- 80"-long 4 × 4 post
- 35¾" × 79" doors
- 72"

SIDE VIEW

- 15°
- 2 × 4 blocking
- 20½" rafter
- 90⅛" 2 × 4
- 79" 4 × 6 beam
- 72"
- 80" 4 × 4 post
- 58"
- 42"
- 30"
- 15½"

FLOOR ASSEMBLY

- 2 × 4 frame under floor
- 1½" × 3½" notch in plywood for rear 2 × 4 and front post
- 13½"
- 79"

Recycling Center

D E S I G N E R ' S   S K E T C H B O O K

It's easy to close the back door and pretend that the jumble of recycling bins and garbage cans outside doesn't exist—but that only works when you're in the house. Building a short lean-to just big enough to hold everything solves the problem.

The key to this design is a pressure-treated 2 by 4 ledger that's screwed to the house wall; additional 2 by 4s and 4 by 4 posts form the side walls and center divider. The rafters are also cut from 2 by 4s. Both the shelves and sheathing are 1/2-inch exterior plywood. Redwood siding and battens cap the sides; additional trim caps the rafters and roof edges.

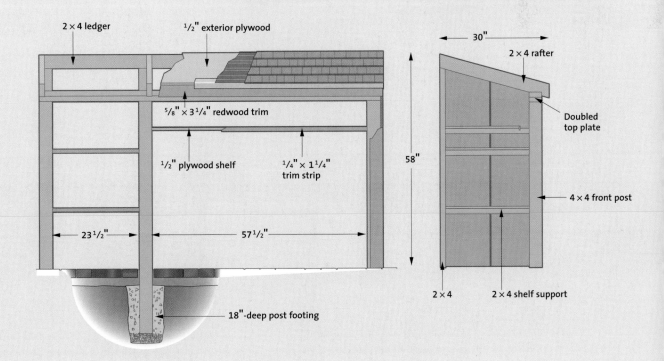

2 × 4 ledger

1/2" exterior plywood

5/8" × 3 1/4" redwood trim

1/2" plywood shelf

1/4" × 1 1/4" trim strip

23 1/2"

57 1/2"

18"-deep post footing

30"

2 × 4 rafter

Doubled top plate

58"

4 × 4 front post

2 × 4

2 × 4 shelf support

GABLE SHED WITH STORAGE BAY

FROM THE FRONT, this classic shed conceals its "secret": a covered storage bay in the rear. Use it to store a cord of firewood, or divide it up to accommodate a protected area for a potting bench or workbench. For a look at the bay, see the photo on page 17. (To purchase plans for this project, see page 159.)

Design Details

This design has a more complex eave treatment than the basic gable shed and includes a doubled beam in back that supports the roof above the storage bay. Nevertheless, this is a straightforward design that can be built in a few weekends.

The 10- by 12-foot structure is designed to be constructed on a slab foundation, but it can also be erected atop poured footings and a framed floor. The highly sloped roof (a 12-in-12 pitch) easily sheds water and snow, and the eaves extend out to shield the gable siding from the elements.

T1-11 siding is used here, but if you add ½-inch plywood sheathing, you could opt for board-and-batten or lap siding. (See pages 50–51 for more on siding options.)

DESIGN: GARLINGHOUSE COMPANY

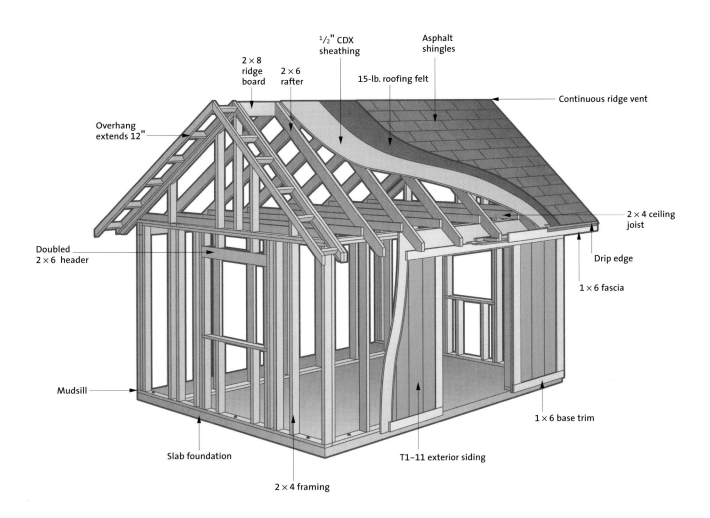

2 × 8 ridge board

2 × 6 rafter

1/2" CDX sheathing

15-lb. roofing felt

Asphalt shingles

Continuous ridge vent

Overhang extends 12"

2 × 4 ceiling joist

Doubled 2 × 6 header

Drip edge

1 × 6 fascia

1 × 6 base trim

Mudsill

Slab foundation

T1–11 exterior siding

2 × 4 framing

Materials List

• Crushed stone		• Corner trim, door and window trim, frieze boards	1 × 4
• Vapor retarder	6 mil	• Soffit nailers	2 × 2
• Rebar	#5	• Plywood soffits	3/8"
• Welded wire mesh	6 × 6	• Soffit vents	
• Concrete		• Ridge vent, drip edge, 15-lb. roofing felt	
• Anchor bolts		• Asphalt shingles	
• Pressure-treated mudsills	2 × 4	• Windows	3'0" × 3'0"
• Wall studs, sills, double top plates, trimmer studs, cripple studs, gable overhangs, gable studs, ceiling joists	2 × 4	• Prehung double door	4'0" × 6'8"
		• Base trim and fascia	1 × 6
• Doubled beams and ridge board	2 × 8	• Beam trim	1 × 10
• Headers and rafters	2 × 6	• Metal framing brackets and fasteners	
• T1-11 exterior siding	5/8"	• Galvanized nails and outdoor screws	
• CDX roof sheathing	1/2"	• Paint or stain	

How to Build the Gable Shed with Storage Bay

Be sure to study the step-by-step photos showing the construction of this shed in Chapter Three, "Building Basics." The most challenging parts of this project are adding the overhang on the gables and trimming out the soffits at the eaves. In addition, you'll have the opportunity to cut a true rafter, bird's mouth and all. Expect this to be a trial-and-error process until you get two rafters that fit just right.

1 **POUR THE SLAB.** The slab foundation shown here uses rebar and welded wire mesh for reinforcement (see foundation detail at right). Place anchor bolts 6 inches from the corners and centered along the 10-foot width of the slab. Press them into the wet concrete 2 inches in from the edges. On the door side of the slab, place anchors 9 inches in from each corner, and put two additional anchors 6 inches from each side of the door opening. Along the back wall, which is 2 feet in from the edge of the slab, space another three anchors. Place an additional anchor 11 inches in from the back edge of the slab to hold the storage bay's central partition wall.

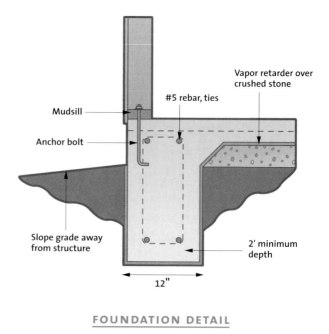

FOUNDATION DETAIL

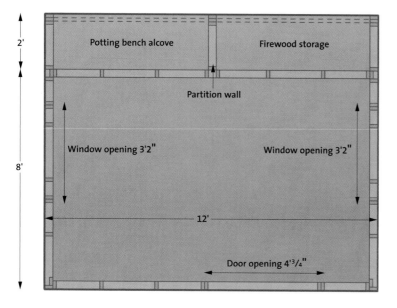

FLOOR PLAN

2 **BUILD THE WALLS.** Cut pressure-treated 2 by 4 mudsills to length, mark the anchor locations, and drill holes. Cut top plates to length and lay out wall studs 24 inches on center on matched pairs of mudsills and top plates. Note that the side walls each have two additional shorter end studs in back to support a doubled 2 by 8 beam over the storage bay. The small partition wall for the bay tucks below the beam. Lay out rough openings for the door and windows, and assemble headers. Then build each wall, adding trimmer studs, headers, sills, and cripple studs as needed.

3 **RAISE THE WALLS.** Lift each wall so that the mudsill fits over the anchor bolts. Place washers over the bolts and thread on nuts but do not fully tighten. Brace each wall as necessary. Bridge the back ends of the side walls with a 12-foot-long 2 by 8, add a second 2 by 8, and nail the two together at the ends and every 16 inches or so to form the beam. After checking the walls for level and plumb, nail them together at the corners. Then tighten the nuts on the mudsills. Cut and install the double top plates and also cut out the mudsill at the door opening.

4 **FRAME THE ROOF.** The roof is framed with 2 by 6 rafters, a 2 by 8 ridge board, and 2 by 4 ceiling joists. Using the pattern shown at right, cut a pair of rafters; then test the fit as described on page 76. Use your best rafter as a template to cut the rest. Next, lay out the ridge board

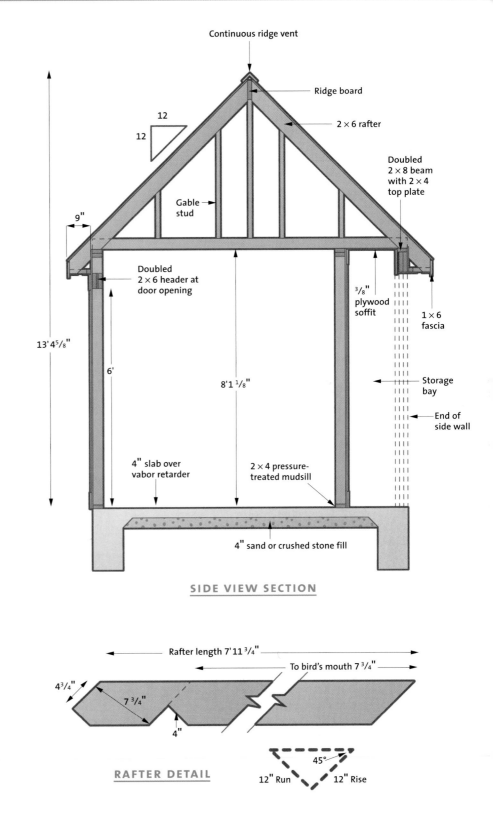

SIDE VIEW SECTION

RAFTER DETAIL

for 24-inch on-center rafters, and transfer these locations to the top plates. Attach a pair of rafters to each end of the ridge board, then lift this structure up onto the top plates. Cut a center gable stud and toenail it in place; repeat for the opposite end. Install the other rafters. Then cut and install the gable overhang framing shown on page 105 (these pieces are cut much like rafters); this "ladder" is then attached to the end rafters.

continued ▶▶

5 **FRAME THE GABLE END.** Cut gable studs to fit directly above the wall studs. To lay them out, use a level to align each gable stud and then mark and cut the top angle. Toenail the gable studs in place. Cut and install the ceiling joists.

6 **ENCLOSE THE SHED.** Cut sheets of T1-11 siding so that the edges meet on studs. Attach the siding with galvanized 8d nails placed approximately every 8 inches. Cover the roof framing with 1/2-inch CDX plywood sheathing.

7 **TRIM OUT THE OVERHANGS.** Before shingling the roof, it's best to add the fascia and soffit trim (see rafter and eave details below). Cut and install the 1 by 6 eave fascia, a 2 by 2 continuous soffit nailer, and 2 by 2 framing between the continuous nailer and each rafter tail. Cut and install soffit vents and the 3/8-inch plywood soffits. Add additional soffits below the gable overhangs and finish up with 1 by 6 rake trim.

8 **APPLY THE ROOFING.** Add a layer of 15-pound roofing felt on top of the sheathing and install drip edge along the gables and eaves. Install a continuous ridge vent, then apply asphalt shingles and ridge caps. (See pages 78–79 for more on roofing.)

9 **INSTALL A DOOR AND WINDOWS.** Shim the windows for level and plumb and attach them with galvanized nails or screws. Then install the prehung double-door unit. (If prehung double doors are unavailable, make your own set from a pair of single doors or 3/4-inch exterior plywood and 2 by 2 framing.)

10 **ADD FINAL TRIM.** Cut and attach base trim, corner boards, frieze boards (the horizontal trim on each gable side), and door and window trim. Finally, cut and install trim across the inside face of the beam and along the joints where soffits meet walls.

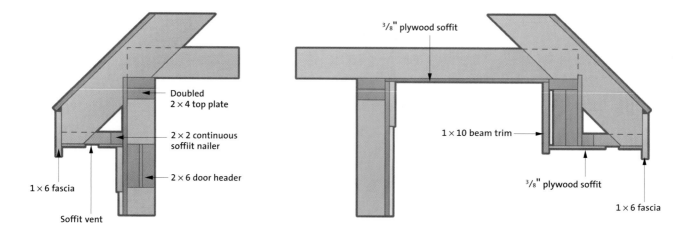

Doubled
2 × 4 top plate

2 × 2 continuous
soffiit nailer

2 × 6 door header

1 × 6 fascia

Soffit vent

3/8" plywood soffit

1 × 10 beam trim

3/8" plywood soffit

1 × 6 fascia

RAFTER AND EAVE DETAIL

Simply Small

Second only to a lean-to (see pages 98–103), a gable shed like this one is wonderfully easy to build. Add shutters, window boxes, and a Dutch door, vary the siding a bit, and you have a nicely detailed project that belies its uncomplicated origins. Use it for storage or turn it into a playhouse, mini-office, or poolside cabana.

Because of its small size, this shed won't require a heavy-duty foundation; it can rest on skids, blocks, or precast concrete piers. The basic design is easy to enlarge or reduce.

DESIGN: SUMMERWOOD PRODUCTS

The gable roof is built with simple trusses, which ease roof assembly and make for a very solid structure. For truss-making tips, see page 149. The roof frame can be covered with plywood sheathing and asphalt shingles (shown) or with spaced sheathing and cedar shingles or shakes (page 123).

To purchase this shed in kit form, see page 159.

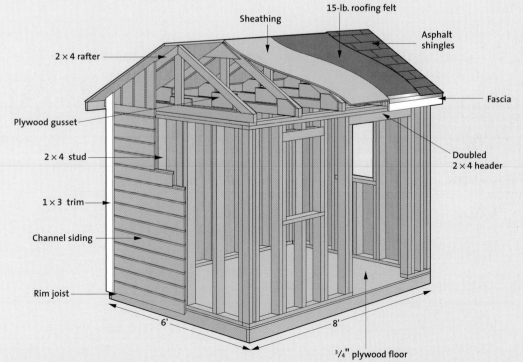

Norwegian Cabin

DESIGNER'S SKETCHBOOK

Designed to be a playhouse now and a potting shed later, this tiny cottage was inspired by a family's memories of several years spent in Norway. Like many a Scandinavian outbuilding, the playhouse has a sod roof and a board ceiling. Other homespun details include recycled leaded-glass windows, two of which were kitchen cabinet doors in their first life, and a Dutch door, which was fashioned from an old two-panel door.

The roof's peak isn't very high because sod would slide off a steep slope. To keep things kid-size but still provide some headroom for adults, the carpenter who designed

DESIGN: BOB STANTON

and built the structure skipped the usual roof rafters or trusses. Instead, the roof is supported by three hefty beams, one at the ridge and two over the side walls. Over those he nailed car decking, 2 by 6 boards with tongue-and-groove edges. Their interlocking design adds strength and stability.

He further strengthened the structure by nailing a few of the roof boards to the top framing piece on the front and back walls, adding diagonal bracing, and notching studs into the top plate of each wall. To form the ⅝-inch-deep notches, first make multiple passes with a circular saw, leaving about ⅛ inch between cuts. A chisel quickly cleans out the waste (see photo below). The added joinery gives the structure some of the feel of a timber-frame building.

A plastic pond liner big enough to cover the entire roof serves as a waterproof membrane. A dimpled plastic sheet, sold primarily for water-proofing basements, is laid over that. Then two layers of turf, one placed grass side down and the other grass side up, are rolled out. The plastic sheet's dimples create an airspace on the back and give the grass roots something to grip on the front. Parallel grooves formed in the plastic point downhill, channeling rainwater off the roof.

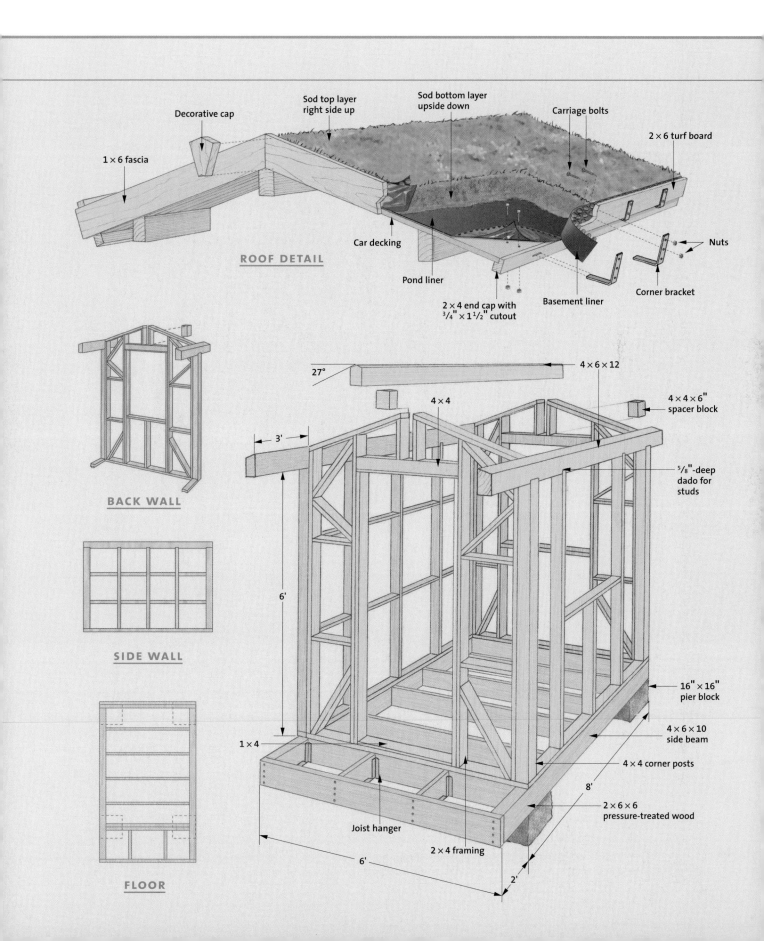

ROOF DETAIL

Decorative cap

Sod top layer right side up

Sod bottom layer upside down

Carriage bolts

2 × 6 turf board

1 × 6 fascia

Nuts

Car decking

Pond liner

Corner bracket

2 × 4 end cap with $\frac{3}{4}" \times 1\frac{1}{2}"$ cutout

Basement liner

BACK WALL

SIDE WALL

FLOOR

27°

4 × 6 × 12

4 × 4

4 × 4 × 6" spacer block

3'

$\frac{5}{8}"$-deep dado for studs

6'

16" × 16" pier block

1 × 4

4 × 6 × 10 side beam

4 × 4 corner posts

8'

2 × 6 × 6 pressure-treated wood

Joist hanger

2 × 4 framing

6'

2'

DESIGN: KEVIN DOWN, NORTHERN PINE SHEDS

SALTBOX SHED

FOR A TRULY RURAL SILHOUETTE, consider the saltbox shed. The main benefit of this classic design is headroom. Almost as soon as you enter, you can stand up straight to use the ample space inside. This 8- by 12-foot version features a ramp and double doors for stowing lawn and garden equipment. Cedar board-and-batten siding accentuates the simple lines that make this design enormously popular.

1 × 10 roof boards

2 × 6 ridge board

2 × 6 rafters

15-lb. roofing felt

Asphalt shingles

2 × 4 collar tie

1 × 6 fascia

1 × 6 fascia

4 × 6 corner post

Rafter tie

Top plate

2 × 4 middle rail

4 × 4 pressure-treated floor frame

1 × 10 floor boards

4 × 4 door post

1 × 3 batten

1 × 10 pine siding

Design Details

This stout shed uses timber framing techniques (often called post-and-beam construction). But don't worry, there's no fancy mortise-and-tenon joinery here—the large beams are simply nailed together. The strength comes from nailing 1 by 10 siding to the beams to create a surprisingly rigid structure.

Although the design calls for double doors, it can easily be modified for a single door. Also, because of the post-and-beam construction, you can install as many windows as you like on any or all sides of the shed. Note that although the door posts and top plates call for 4 by 4 beams, you can safely substitute doubled 2 by 4s nailed together every 6 inches or so.

Materials List

• Concrete and pea gravel for footings	
• Pressure-treated beams for floor frame	4 × 4
• Floor boards	1 × 10
• Corner posts	4 × 6
• Top plates and door posts	4 × 4
• Middle rails and collar ties	2 × 4
• Ridge board and rafters	2 × 6
• Siding boards	1 × 10
• Siding battens	1 × 3
• Roof boards	1 × 10
• Drip edge and 15-lb. roofing felt	
• Asphalt shingles and ridge caps	
• Sliding windows	2'0" by 2'0"
• Fascia	1 × 6
• Corner, window, and door trim	1 × 3
• Galvanized nails	
• Metal post anchors (optional)	
• Metal framing brackets and fasteners	
• Strap hinges and door latch	
• Paint, stain, or water sealer	

How to Build the Saltbox Shed

Most of this shed is built with straightforward stick-framing techniques. The one exception is the timber-framed walls: Be sure to have at least one strong helper on hand to handle the heavy 4 by 4s and 4 by 6s. If you're not great at toenailing (page 71), consider making these post-and-beam connections with metal framing connectors (page 47).

1 INSTALL THE FLOOR. The foundation for this shed can be skids, concrete piers, or poured footings (pages 62–63). The floor frame is 4 by 4 pressure-treated pine; the long pieces are 12 feet long, and the ends and joists are 7 feet 5 inches long. Together they make an 8- by 12-foot frame.

Connect the frame by toenailing parts together, or use joist hangers; 4 by 4 joists are spaced 24 inches on center. Place the finished frame on the footings, shim it level, and secure it to the footings. To cover the frame, cut 12-foot-long 1 by 10s and use 8d nails to secure them to the frame (alternatively, use ¾-inch tongue-and-groove plywood).

2 BUILD THE WALLS. First, cut four 4 by 6 corner posts to 75 inches long. Next, cut the long front and back top plates to 12 feet and lay out the rafter locations 24 inches on center; mark the rafter locations on the 12-foot-long 2 by 6 ridge board as well. Then cut the two shorter side top plates to 7 feet 5 inches long. Secure the corner posts to the floor framing with nails or metal angle brackets (no bottom plates are required). Brace these posts in place (page 73). Then rest the top plates on the posts and either toenail them or use framing connectors and face-nail them. Cut the

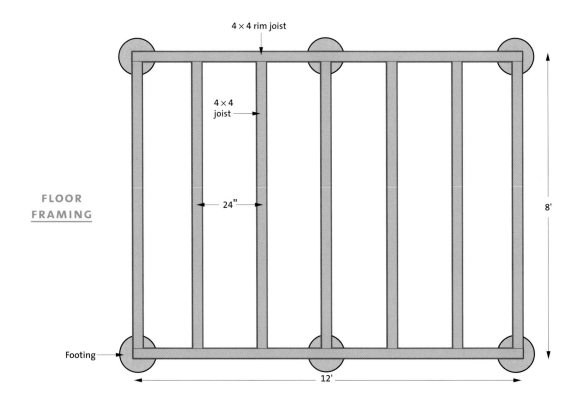

4 × 4 rim joist

4 × 4 joist

24"

FLOOR
FRAMING

8'

Footing

12'

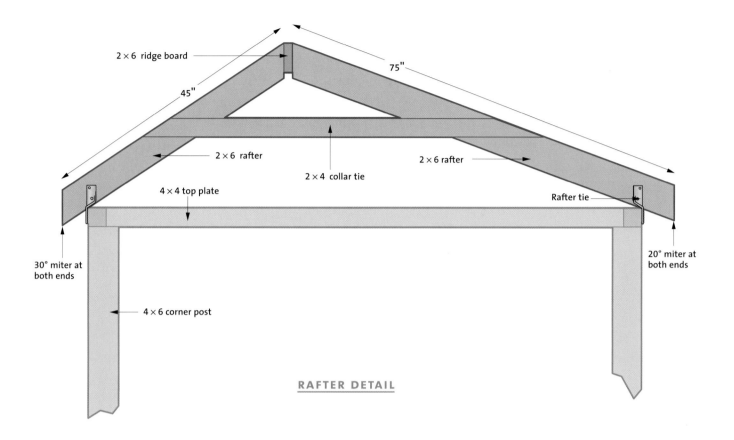

2 × 6 ridge board

45"

75"

2 × 6 rafter

2 × 6 rafter

2 × 4 collar tie

4 × 4 top plate

Rafter tie

30° miter at
both ends

20° miter at
both ends

4 × 6 corner post

RAFTER DETAIL

4 by 4 door posts to 75 inches long and install. Level and plumb the walls and add temporary diagonal bracing inside the shed from post to post to keep it square. Measure, cut, and attach the 2 by 4 middle rails 36 inches up from the floor.

3 **ENCLOSE THE WALL FRAME.** Cut 1 by 10 siding boards to 81 ½ inches for the eave sides and attach them flush with the top plates. Next, cut 1 by 10 gable boards 10 feet long so they'll run "wild" on top (they'll be cut to length after the rafters are up).

4 **FRAME THE ROOF.** Temporarily attach the ridge board to the gable siding. It should be 32 inches in from the front of the shed and 26 inches up from the top plate. Then cut

pairs of short and long rafters as shown in the rafter detail above. With a helper, hold a pair of rafters up against the ridge board and gable siding, and scribe the rafter outline onto the siding; cut along the marked line with a circular saw or a reciprocating saw. Repeat at the opposite end. Attach the end rafters to the ridge board, top plate, and siding. Nail the remaining rafters to the ridge board and secure their opposite ends to the top plates with rafter ties. Brace the rafters with 55-inch-long 2 by 4 collar ties.

5 **APPLY SHEATHING AND ROOFING.** For roof sheathing, use 1 by 10 boards or ¾-inch CDX plywood, starting at the bottom and working up toward the ridge. Add drip edge and 15-pound roofing felt. Install asphalt shingles and ridge caps. (See pages 78–79 for more details on roofing.)

continued ▶▶

6 **INSTALL WINDOWS AND DOORS.** Mark window locations in the siding and cut out the openings with a reciprocating saw or a jigsaw. Attach each flanged window with galvanized nails or outdoor screws and trim it with 1 by 3s. Cut and nail on corner trim and door trim. Next, cover the seams between siding boards with 1 by 3 battens, fitting them around the door and window trim. Also cut and attach 1 by 6 fascia to the ends of the rafters, and add rake trim at the gable ends.

Using 1 by 10 shiplap boards, 1 by 10s, and 1 by 3s, build a pair of doors to fit the opening (see below). Attach the doors with strap hinges, then install a door latch. If desired, add screening between the ends of the rafters and the top plates to keep out insects.

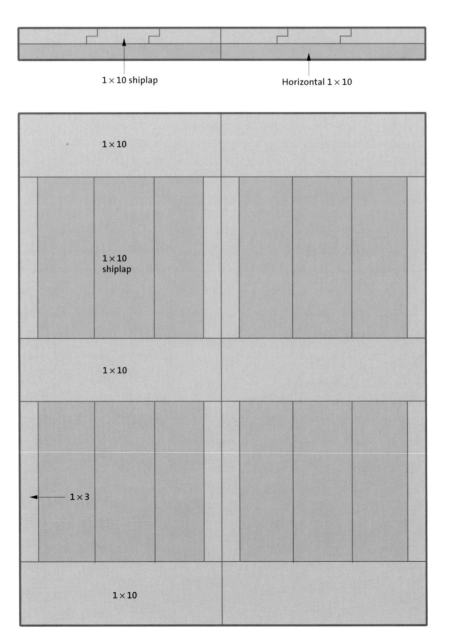

1 × 10 shiplap   Horizontal 1 × 10

1 × 10

1 × 10
shiplap

1 × 10

1 × 3

1 × 10

DOOR DETAIL

Custom Concepts

Hips, valleys, and other roof planes can be tough to design and frame. However, there's another, simpler trick for creating custom shapes and rooflines: Just join two or more basic sheds together!

For example, the clerestory shed shown at right is really two shed-roof, or lean-to, structures joined back to back: one extra-tall main shed slopes in one direction, and a shorter lean-to runs the other way. The net effect is a bit like a saltbox profile. The two wings share a wall—in the large drawing, a wide doorway formed by a long header allows you to pass from one space to the other. The top of the shared wall is the perfect spot for a bank of clerestory windows, bringing welcome light to the interior space that's blocked by the front shed.

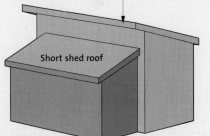

Clerestory windows

Shared wall

A second common style, especially popular for barns, is shown below right. It's based on a tall central gable-roof structure, with one or two shed-roof wings branching off the main structure's eave walls. A third sketch below shows two gables, one big and one small, joined end to end; the shorter structure can serve as an entryway, porch, or work/storage annex. You could also join the sheds at right angles, but it's harder to keep the rooflines apart unless the main structure is pretty tall.

You can, of course, also use this multiplying strategy to expand your new shed, garage, or barn later.

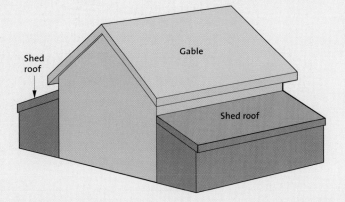

Tall shed roof

Short shed roof

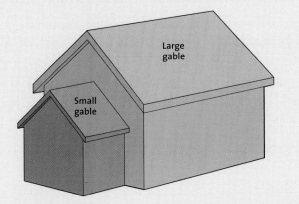

Large gable

Small gable

Shed roof

Gable

Shed roof

DESIGN: SUMMERWOOD PRODUCTS

HIP-ROOF SHED

WHETHER THIS SHED HOUSES garden tools or a poolside changing room, its lines lend a touch of formality to the structure's functionality. Since the hip-roof overhang surrounds the structure, eaves offer unbroken protection. The distinctive roofline is a construction challenge—but could be a great way for a budding carpenter to gain some new skills. To purchase the shed in kit form, see page 159.

Design Details

The version of the shed illustrated on the facing page measures 8 by 12 feet, but the simple floor and wall framing can be revised easily for a smaller footprint. The framing of the hip roof, on the other hand, is complex and potentially frustrating for a first-time builder. (For more on hip roofs, see page 74.) If you're not comfortable framing the roof, consider hiring out that portion of the job. Once the roof is framed and installed, the sheathing and roofing are easy to install.

   Note: This hip-roof shed has a shorter profile than some other structures—the eaves are just 76½ inches off the floor. If you'd prefer a taller entryway and a standard-height door, plan to substitute longer wall studs. (For wall-framing details, see pages 70–73.)

Materials List

- Pressure-treated skids   4 × 6
- Pressure-treated rim/floor joists   2 × 6
- Top and bottom plates, wall studs, sills, headers, trimmer studs, cripple studs, common and jack rafters   2 × 4
- Tongue-and-groove plywood flooring   ³⁄₄"
- Ridge board and hip rafters   2 × 6
- 4-light windows (optional)   2'0" × 2'4"
- Prehung door unit or exterior door, jambs, hinges, and threshold to fit   3'0" wide

- CDX roof sheathing   ⁵⁄₈"
- Drip edge and 15-lb. roofing felt
- Asphalt shingles and ridge caps
- Cedar channel siding   ³⁄₄" × 6"
- Cedar soffits, fascia, corner trim, door and window casing   1 × 4
- Galvanized nails and outdoor screws
- Metal framing brackets and fasteners
- Paint, stain, or water sealer

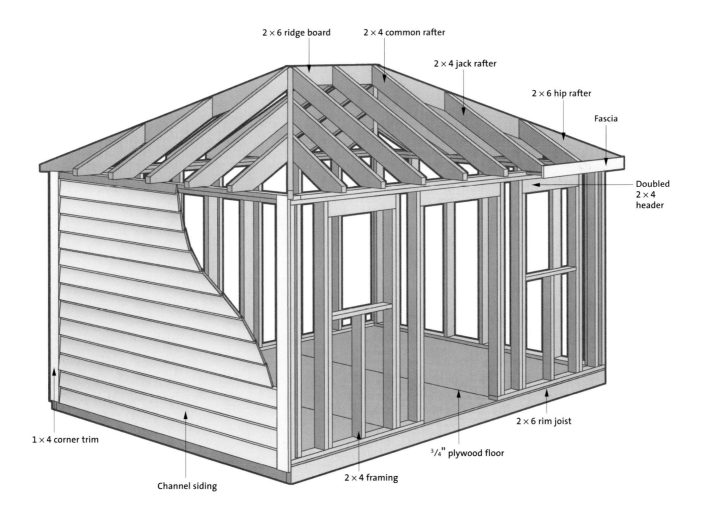

2 × 6 ridge board · 2 × 4 common rafter · 2 × 4 jack rafter · 2 × 6 hip rafter · Fascia · Doubled 2 × 4 header · 2 × 6 rim joist · ³⁄₄" plywood floor · 2 × 4 framing · Channel siding · 1 × 4 corner trim

How to Build the Hip-roof Shed

This project is mostly straightforward to build—with the notable exception of the hip roof. The easiest solution here is to build the roof frame on the shed floor before erecting the walls. Then, with the aid of some strong helpers, the framed roof can be lifted onto the completed walls.

1 **INSTALL THE FOUNDATION.** This shed can be built atop skids, concrete piers, poured footings, or a concrete slab. If you choose skids for a foundation, use three 12-foot-long 4 by 6 pressure-treated beams, one centered from front to back and the other two 42 inches to each side. (For details on other foundations, see pages 62–67.) If you opt for a concrete slab, you can leave off the floor framing in Step 2 and attach pressure-treated mudsills directly to the slab with anchor bolts.

2 **FRAME THE FLOOR.** Build the floor frame by first cutting two rim joists 12 feet long. Mark positions for the joists 16 inches on center and cut them 93 inches long. Attach them to the rim joists with 16d nails or joist hangers. Position the frame atop the skids and shim it level; check the diagonals, and when the frame is square, toe-nail it in place. Cover with $^3/_4$-inch tongue-and-groove plywood, fastening it with 8d galvanized nails or 2-inch outdoor screws.

3 **FRAME THE ROOF.** The simplest way to frame the roof is to build it on the floor frame before the walls are erected and then place it on the shed when complete. The roof pitch is 7 in 12. To start, cut a double set of top plates and temporarily attach one set around the perimeter of the floor frame with screws; also fasten the ends together with $3^1/_2$-inch outdoor screws.

Mark the center of each side frame and the center of the ridge board. Cut and attach the six common rafters for the front and back, notching the ends to fit over the top plates. Attach the two common rafters to the ends of the ridge board and to the top plates. Cut and install the four hip rafters

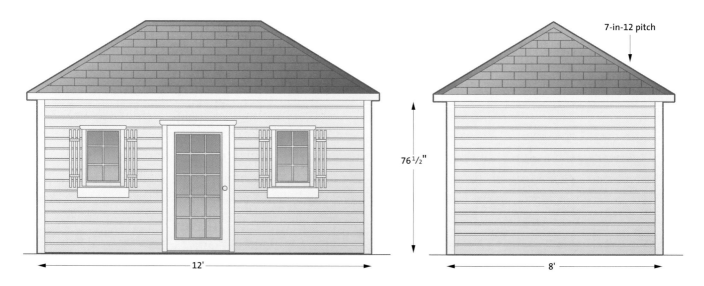

7-in-12 pitch

76$^1/_2$"

12'

8'

FRONT ELEVATION

SIDE ELEVATION

angled from the corners of the walls to the ridge board. Cut and attach the 16 jack rafters; ends connecting to the hip rafters will have to be mitered to match the hip rafter angle. Remove the screws holding the framed roof in place and set the roof aside.

4 **FRAME THE WALLS.** To build each wall section, first cut a set of bottom plates to match the top plates you've already cut. Then measure and mark the positions of the wall studs and rough openings. Cut enough wall studs 72 inches long for 16-inch-on-center spacing, and assemble each wall. Frame rough openings by adding trimmer studs, headers, cripple studs, and sills as required.

5 **RAISE AND SECURE THE WALLS.** Set the first wall on the floor, and secure it by driving screws through the bottom plate into the floor frame. Brace the wall temporarily (page 73), and raise and secure the remaining wall sections in the same way. Check for plumb, and secure the walls to each other at the corners.

6 **ADD THE ROOF.** Before attaching the framed roof to the shed, it's easiest to first precut ⅝-inch sheathing to cover the frame. Label all pieces and set them aside. With the help of four strong helpers, lift the framed roof onto the shed walls. Secure the roof frame to the walls by screwing down through the attached top plates into the top plates of the walls. Add the precut sheathing, drip edge, roofing felt, shingles, and ridge caps. (For roofing details, see pages 78–79.)

ROOF FRAMING DETAIL

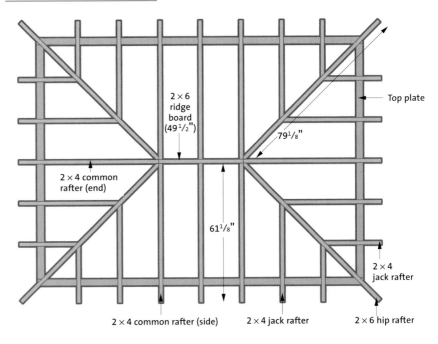

2 × 6 ridge board (49½")

2 × 4 common rafter (end)

79⅛"

Top plate

61⅛"

2 × 4 jack rafter

2 × 4 common rafter (side)   2 × 4 jack rafter   2 × 6 hip rafter

7 **APPLY SIDING AND TRIM.** Note: If you're using flanged windows, install them before you apply the siding; otherwise, install the windows afterward. Cut and install cedar channel siding horizontally, starting from the bottom and working to the top plate. Allow the bottom edge of the first piece of siding to overhang the bottom plate by ¾ inch. Cut and install the soffits, fascia, and corner trim.

8 **INSTALL THE DOOR.** If you're building this shed as is, you'll probably need to cut a standard door down to size or make one of your own—the height of the door opening is only about 70 inches. If a prehung door won't work, you'll need a top jamb and two side jambs to line the opening; secure an exterior door to the jamb with butt hinges. (For more details on doors, see pages 84–85.) Also add a separate threshold if required. Install a door latch or doorset. Finally, trim around the door and windows, and add shutter trim if desired.

GREENHOUSE SHED

IS IT A GREENHOUSE? A storage shed? An art studio? A workshop? The answer is yes and then some when you opt for this versatile, light-filled structure. The clear glazing of the greenhouse window panels, plus the functional double Dutch door and standard rear window, ensure ample air and light for any use. (To purchase this shed in kit form, see page 159.)

Design Details

This 8- by 12-foot saltbox shed gives you the option of orienting the largest portion of the roof to the south for maximum light and heat. However, orienting the shed northward will still provide plenty of indirect light.

The greenhouse windows are sheets of $\frac{1}{4}$-inch Lexan (polycarbonate). The seams are sealed with self-adhesive foam tape and covered with Lexan strips that are screwed to the roof frame.

Although this stick-framed shed design calls for 2 by 3 framing lumber, you may prefer to use conventional 2 by 4s. If you do, be sure to compensate for the added width as you build.

DESIGN: CEDARSHED INDUSTRIES, INC.

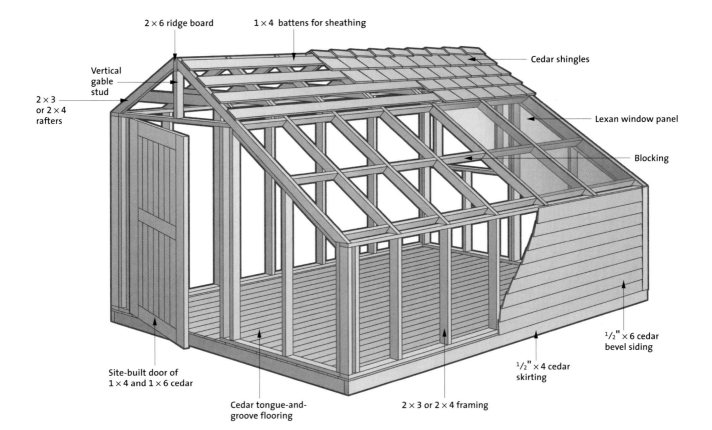

2 × 6 ridge board

1 × 4 battens for sheathing

Cedar shingles

Vertical gable stud

2 × 3 or 2 × 4 rafters

Lexan window panel

Blocking

Site-built door of 1 × 4 and 1 × 6 cedar

Cedar tongue-and-groove flooring

2 × 3 or 2 × 4 framing

¹/₂" × 4 cedar skirting

¹/₂" × 6 cedar bevel siding

Materials List

- Precast concrete piers or concrete for footings
- Floor joists 2 × 6
- Tongue-and-groove cedar or pine flooring or tongue-and-groove plywood flooring ³/₄"
- Top and bottom plates and wall studs 2 × 3 or 2 × 4
- Collar ties, rafters, and blocking 2 × 3 or 2 × 4
- Ridge board 2 × 6
- Lexan window panels, cover strips, foam tape, screws, and neoprene washers
- Open roof sheathing 1 × 4
- Cedar roofing shingles and ridge caps

- Window 2'0" × 2'4"
- Door 1 × 6, 1 × 4
- Door hinges and doorset
- Cedar door and window wrap 1 × 6
- Cedar bevel siding ¹/₂" × 6"
- Cedar top, skirting, and soffits ¹/₂" × 4"
- Cedar corner trim and bottom skirting 1 × 4
- Fascia 1 × 4
- Vertical battens 1 × 2
- Galvanized nails or joist hangers and outdoor screws
- Metal framing brackets and fasteners
- Paint, stain, or water sealer

How to Build the Greenhouse Shed

This project offers plenty of wrinkles: saltbox roof, greenhouse glazing, cedar shingles, Dutch doors, and lap siding. The biggest challenges are cutting and assembling the angled side walls and offset rafters. If you'd like to outfit your greenhouse shed with potting benches or tables, see the easy-to-build ideas on pages 157–159.

1 **FRAME THE FLOOR.** The floor framing rests on concrete piers or poured footings spaced approximately every 4 feet. To build the frame, mark joist locations 16 inches on center on two 12-foot rim joists. Then cut 12 floor joists to a length of 93 inches each and attach them to the rim joists with 16d nails or joist hangers. With helpers on hand, position the frame on the piers or footings, then level it as needed with shims. Cover the framing with tongue-and-groove pine or cedar flooring or ¾-inch plywood.

2 **BUILD THE WALLS.** Cut top and bottom plates, each 12 feet long, for the high rear and low front walls. Then cut wall studs: seven that are 37¼ inches long and seven more that are 71¾ inches long. Lay out the wall studs 24 inches on center and build the two walls. Next, cut plates and studs for the side walls. The bottom plates are 89 inches long, and the top plates 46½ inches. The studs are 73⅛ inches, 59⁹⁄₁₆ inches, and 39³⁄₁₆ inches long, starting from the tall end; the two shorter studs are angled at 36½ degrees on top to match the pitch of the roof. Frame the rough openings for the door (36 inches wide) and window (26 inches by 30 inches).

continued ▶▶

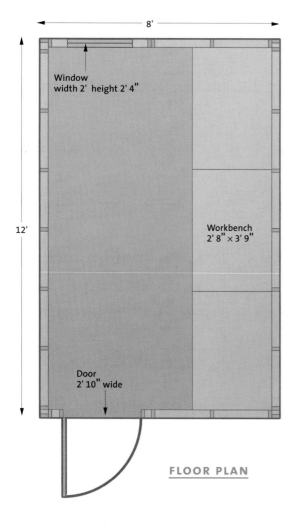

FLOOR PLAN

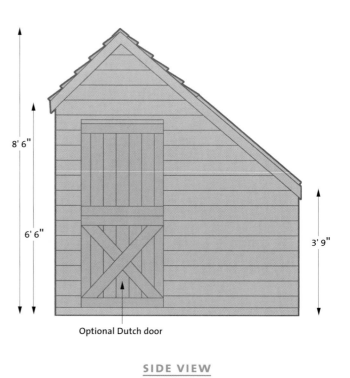

SIDE VIEW

Little House on the Patio

Sometimes, one thing leads to another. For instance, this potting shed started with an unusable slope. The architect, an avid gardener, first created a level terrace and installed a patio. Then he used the patio as the platform to build the little house shown at right.

To facilitate construction, he made it 8 feet square, which allowed him to use standard 8-foot materials; he cut the door down to 6 feet.

So that the shed would last a long time, he wanted to use the most rotproof materials he could find. For the walls, he chose 1/2-inch cement backerboard instead of plywood, and for the floor, concrete patio blocks. Standard stud-and-joist framing rests on pressure-treated 4 by 6 skids, which serve as footings for the load-bearing side walls.

The roof is covered with asphalt shingles. Gutters channel rainwater into a 44-gallon plastic trash container, which serves as a cistern supplying the sink inside. The flower-filled window boxes, irrigated with the rainwater, are made from 1/4-inch backerboard screwed onto a cedar frame.

DESIGN: BARI THOMPSON

Potting with Pizzazz

Planted in a flower and vegetable patch, this garden center looks like a diminutive English cottage, where Peter Rabbit might feel at home. The structure is 10 feet long by 88 inches wide and only 91 inches tall. The lower edge of the roof is about 5 feet at its highest point; to make a human-size opening, the doorway had to be notched into the shingles. Two 2-foot-square windows and lattice panels under the eaves let light inside. Potting and arranging can be done on a U-shaped counter inside, and the brick-on-sand floor is easily washed down.

DESIGN: LEO SNIDER,
COVENTRY LANDSCAPE

3 **RAISE THE WALLS.** Position the rear wall flush with the floor and screw it to the floor frame, bracing as needed. Repeat this for the front and side walls. Add extra corner studs to the long walls (page 73). Check for level and plumb, then screw the wall sections together at the corners. Before you attach the rafters, lay out their locations 24 inches on center on the top plates.

4 **FRAME THE ROOF.** Start by cutting the rafters to length: The short rafters are $28\frac{13}{16}$ inches long and the long rafters are $86\frac{13}{16}$ inches long. Both the short and long rafters are angled at the peak at $36\frac{1}{2}$ degrees. Attach the end rafters to a 12-foot-long ridge board and place this assembly on the wall frame. Attach the free ends of the rafters to the walls by screwing up through the top plates and into the rafters. Install the remaining rafters along the ridge board. Add short gable-end studs between end rafters and top plates. Cut and install two rows of blocking between the rafters, at 29 and 59 inches up from the short wall. There's also a third row of blocking just above the top plates. Finally, cut and install collar ties and attach them to the rafters.

5 **INSTALL GREENHOUSE GLAZING.** Cut the Lexan: Four pieces are $23\frac{1}{4}$ inches wide by 60 inches long, and two pieces are $24\frac{3}{4}$ inches wide by 60 inches long (these are placed adjacent to the gable ends of the roof). Apply double-sided foam tape the length of the rafters, then remove the plastic protective film from the Lexan and position the panels on the roof frame. Apply foam tape over the seams and cover these with $1\frac{1}{2}$-inch-wide, 60-inch-long Lexan strips, as shown above. Drill $\frac{1}{8}$-inch holes through the strip and into the rafters every 12 inches. Secure with 2-inch screws and neoprene washers.

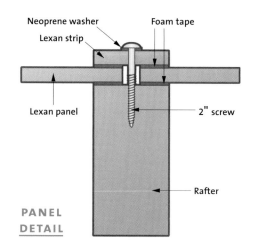

Neoprene washer   Foam tape

Lexan strip

Lexan panel   2" screw

Rafter

PANEL DETAIL

6 **SHINGLE THE ROOF.** The remaining roof area is covered with cedar shingles. Start by cutting and attaching 1 by 4 open sheathing on both sides of the ridge. Install additional 1 by 4s, spacing them apart for the desired shingle exposure. Attach shingles to sheathing, working from the bottom up. Install cap shingles along the ridge.

7 **ADD REAR WINDOW AND DOORS.** First wrap the insides of the window opening with 1 by 6 cedar, nailing it to the surrounding framing. Also wrap the top and sides of the door opening. Install the rear window in its opening. Then build a pair of Dutch doors (see the photo on page 122) or, if you prefer, a single door to fit the opening. Mount the door or doors with butt hinges, then install a latch or doorset.

8 **ENCLOSE THE WALLS.** Apply $\frac{1}{2}$-inch by 6-inch bevel siding, starting at the bottom and working up, using a 1-inch overlap and 6d galvanized nails. Cut and install corner trim, fascia on the ends of rafters, and $\frac{1}{2}$ by 4-inch rake trim along with top and bottom skirting. If you like, finish up with vertical 1 by 2 battens, as shown in the photo on page 122.

Gable Greenhouse

Here's a straightahead gable-roof greenhouse with polycarbonate glazing that starts with standard stud framing. The woodsy redwood and cedar match the look of an adjacent ranch-style home from the 1940s. The southern exposure provides plenty of sun—but it also requires some extra venting in summer.

DESIGN: MICHAEL BOND

The greenhouse sits atop a T-shaped perimeter foundation, which smooths out the slope and provides a "curb" for the gravel floor inside. The owner-builder and a friend built the forms and poured the concrete themselves, working from a trailer of purchased wet mix with a wheelbarrow. The walls and rafters are redwood 2 by 4s; collar ties help brace rafters and provide handy hanging points. The outside skirting was formed by first nailing plywood sheathing across the lower wall studs, covering it with a moisture barrier, then topping that with cedar shingles. A flat cap sits atop the skirt. Pairs of shuttered vents in front and back bring in cooler air as needed.

The upper walls and roof are glazed with polycarbonate panels screwed to the edges of the studs and rafters. A metal ridge vent and drip edge along the gable ends complete the roof. Interior touches include a timer-controlled drip system with spray emitters and lots of built-in benches with slatted tops for drainage.

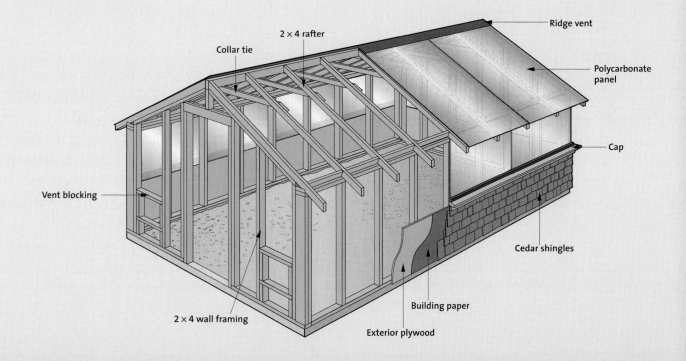

DESIGN: SUMMERWOOD PRODUCTS

FIVE-SIDED CABANA

MAKE SMART USE OF any corner with this distinctive five-sided shed that nestles into the landscape. French doors let in air and light, while optional windows help illuminate the space.

This is a project for experienced carpenters. To purchase the shed in kit form, see page 159.

Design Details

The advantage of a five-sided design is that it's perfect for slipping into a corner. The disadvantage is that the roof framing is tricky. That portion of the project is best tackled by an experienced DIY-er or a professional framer. If you're game, you'll want to rent or buy a compound miter saw to cut the hip-roof rafters and make a neat job of the trim and siding. Fortunately, the floor and wall framing are fairly straightforward.

If you plan to use the shed as a potting shed or workshop, consider adding the optional side windows (shown above). The door framing can be altered to suit either a single door or a set of double doors.

Note: Although this hip-roof shed has ample headroom inside, the eaves are just $76\frac{1}{2}$ inches off the floor. If you'd prefer a taller entryway—and a standard-height door —plan to substitute longer wall studs. (For wall-framing details, see pages 70–73.)

Materials List

- Concrete blocks, precast piers, or concrete for footings
- Pressure-treated mudsills — 2 × 6
- Pressure-treated rim/floor joists — 2 × 6
- Top and bottom plates and wall studs — 2 × 4
- Door header, trimmer studs, cripple studs, and sills — 2 × 4
- Tongue-and-groove plywood flooring — ¾"
- Hip, front, and rear rafters — 2 × 6
- Jack and common rafters — 2 × 4
- CDX roof sheathing — ⅝"

- 6-light windows (optional) — 2'0" × 3'0"
- Double doors (unless built on-site) — 18" wide
- Drip edge and 15-lb. roofing felt
- Asphalt shingles and ridge caps
- Cedar bevel siding — ½" × 6"
- Cedar soffits, fascia, corner and door trim — 1 × 4
- Bottom skirting — 1 × 6
- Galvanized nails and outdoor screws
- Metal framing brackets and fasteners
- Paint, stain, or water sealer

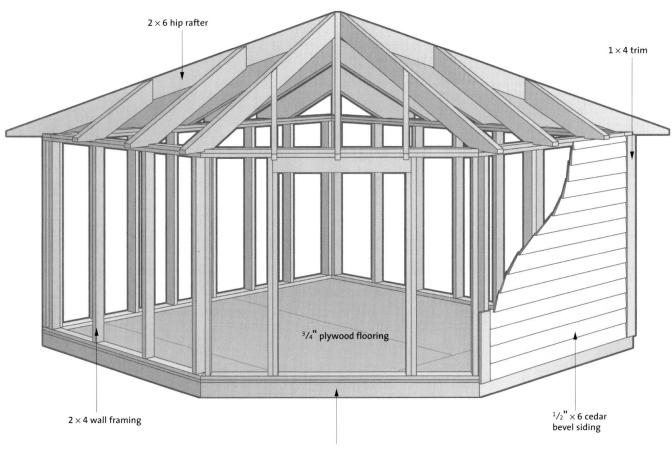

2 × 6 hip rafter

1 × 4 trim

2 × 4 wall framing

¾" plywood flooring

½" × 6 cedar bevel siding

Pressure-treated 2 × 6 joist

How to Build the Five-sided Cabana

The two keys to building this project are laying out the angled foundation and floor frame and assembling the asymmetrical hip roof. Roof framing is best done on the subfloor before the walls are erected. Then the roof can be hoisted onto the walls once they're in place.

1 **INSTALL THE FOUNDATION.** The five-sided cabana can be built atop concrete blocks, precast piers, or permanent poured footings (pages 62–63). These supports should be set in 2 inches along the front wall and two back walls of the shed and spaced roughly 5 feet apart; another set should be centered on the width of the shed. Span the skids, piers, or footings with pressure-treated 2 by 6 mudsills. Alternatively, pour a slab foundation and install anchor bolts around the perimeter for 2 by 4 mudsills.

2 **FRAME THE FLOOR.** Begin by cutting rim joists 120 inches, 117 inches, 85 inches, 60 inches, and 58 ½ inches long. The last three listed have ends angled at 22 ½ degrees, as shown below. Mark floor joist positions 16 inches on center, and cut the joists to length. Attach them to the rim joists with 16d galvanized nails. Position the frame atop the foundation; shim level and toenail in place. Cover the frame with ¾-inch tongue-and-groove plywood, fastening it with 8d galvanized nails or 2-inch outdoor screws.

continued ▶▶

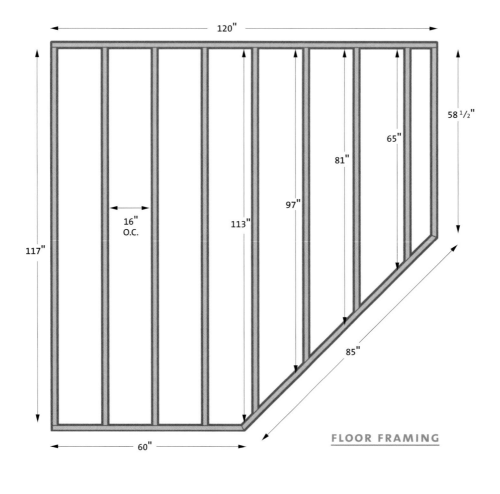

FLOOR FRAMING

Garden Room Gazebo

DESIGNER'S SKETCHBOOK

Looking for a private retreat or dining pavilion? This octagonal garden room is reminiscent of a classic Victorian gazebo, but it cuts a markedly crisper profile. The walls are open to breezes, and an acrylic-sheet skylight adds illumination inside. The skylight can be located in any section of the roof.

The octagonal shape is very efficient at creating maximum space within a minimum perimeter. The interior space provides a full 14 feet of unobstructed room from wall to wall—plenty of space for a dining table and chairs or other furniture.

A great advantage to the framing design is that seven of the eight wall sections are identical. You can measure the pieces for a single section, use them as templates for the others, and cut them all at one time. If you don't own a power miter saw, this project offers the perfect excuse for buying one—it will pay for itself in the labor it saves.

DESIGN: LOU KIMBALL

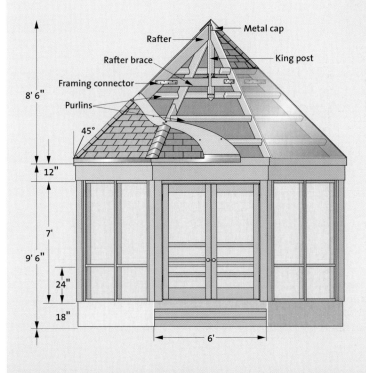

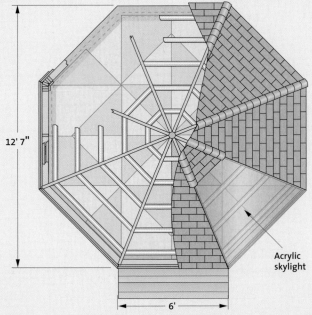

ROOF FRAMING DETAIL

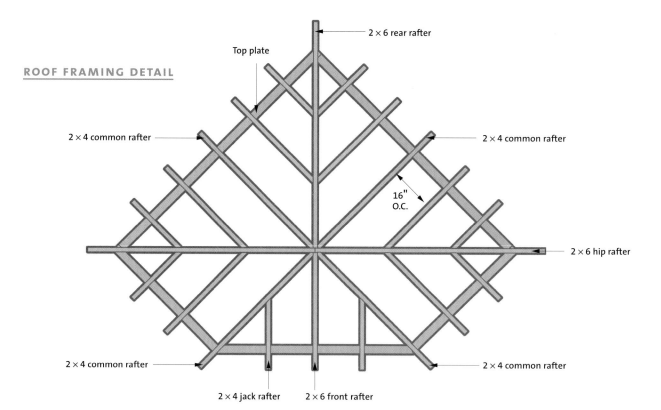

2 × 6 rear rafter

Top plate

2 × 4 common rafter

2 × 4 common rafter

16" O.C.

2 × 6 hip rafter

2 × 4 common rafter

2 × 4 common rafter

2 × 4 jack rafter

2 × 6 front rafter

3 **FRAME THE ROOF.** Although hip roofs can be framed after the walls are raised, you'll find it easier to fit and refit the compound miters of rafters if you frame the roof on the floor and raise it in place later. That way you can attack some very complex framing at a convenient level.

The roof slope is 4 in 12 on the sides and back, and 10 in 12 on the front. Start by cutting a double set of top plates, temporarily attaching one set around the perimeter of the floor frame with screws. Note that the plates for the left and right walls are mitered at 22½ degrees on the ends that connect to the front wall; the ends of the front plate are also mitered. Fasten the ends of the plates together with 3½-inch outdoor screws. Mark the center of each back wall and the front wall.

Cut the two 2 by 6 hip rafters that run from the left corner to the right corner. Cut the top ends at a 4-in-12 slope. Cut

the bottom ends of the rafters to fit over the top plates with a 12-inch overhang. When you are satisfied with the angle cuts, fasten the hip rafters together and temporarily screw them to the top plates. Next, cut and install the front and rear 2 by 6 rafters. After adding 2 by 4 common rafters, install the jack rafters 16 inches on center.

SIDE VIEW

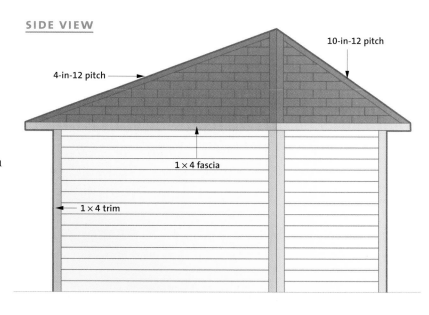

4-in-12 pitch

10-in-12 pitch

1 × 4 fascia

1 × 4 trim

4 **BUILD WALL SECTIONS.** Remove the screws holding the framed roof to the floor and set it aside. Cut bottom plates to match the top plates. Then measure and mark the positions for the wall studs and rough openings. Cut enough wall studs 72 inches long for 16-inch on-center spacing, and assemble each wall. Frame the rough opening by adding the headers, trimmer studs, cripple studs, and sills as required (the door opening is 36½ inches wide and the header snugs right up against the top plate).

5 **RAISE THE WALLS.** Set the right rear wall on the floor and secure it by driving screws through the bottom plate into the floor frame. Brace the wall temporarily (page 73) and then raise the left rear wall, followed by the side walls and the front wall. Check for plumb and secure the walls to each other at the corners.

6 **ADD ROOF SHEATHING.** It's easiest to precut the ⅝-inch roof sheathing now, before attaching the framed roof to the shed. Label all pieces and set them aside. With helpers, lift the framed roof onto the shed walls. Secure it to the walls by screwing down through the attached top plates into the top plates of the walls. Add the sheathing, drip edge, roofing felt, and shingles and ridge caps.

7 **INSTALL DOORS AND WINDOWS.** If you're building this shed as is, you'll probably need to cut a standard set of doors down to size or make two of your own—the height of the door opening is only about 70 inches. (For more details on doors, see pages 84–85.) Add a separate threshold if required.

8 **ADD SIDING AND TRIM.** To enclose the walls, cut and install siding horizontally, starting from the bottom and working to the top plate. Allow the bottom edge of the first piece to overhang the bottom plate by ¾ inch. Cut and install the soffits, fascia, and corner trim. Cover the floor framing with 1 by 6 bottom skirting, then finish up with door trim.

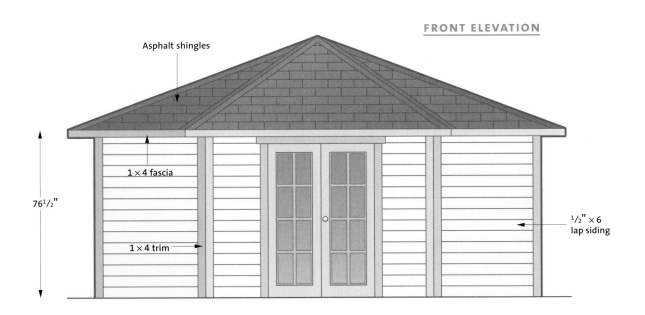

FRONT ELEVATION

Asphalt shingles

1 × 4 fascia

76½"

1 × 4 trim

½" × 6 lap siding

TWO-CAR HIP-ROOF GARAGE

THIS MULTIPURPOSE STRUCTURE offers both flexible space and classic design. The hip roof features complete perimeter overhangs, which protect the structure from weather. Inside, the 24- by 36-foot garage fits two cars, with plenty of extra storage and living or work space.

Design Details

The stick-framed walls are easy to build—the challenge is the hip roof. To simplify things, the designer used preengineered roof trusses, plus a few compound-mitered jack rafters and hip rafters, but you could also use standard hip-roof framing (page 74). If you're not comfortable building the roof, consider hiring out that portion of the job. Once the framing is completed, the sheathing and roofing are straightforward to install.

In addition to the 16-foot-wide overhead door, another 3-foot-wide entrance door should be installed on either side of the garage or along the rear wall. You could easily modify the design to make this a three-car garage by simply adding a second, smaller overhead door in place of the sliding window. If you do this, use a 4 by 12 header and order additional 2 by 6 cedar door wrap.

DESIGN: GARAGES, ETC.

Asphalt shingles

Roofing felt

1/2" CDX sheathing

Common truss

Stepped trusses

Common rafter

1 × 6 fascia

1 × 4 trim

Lap siding

Sliding window

Slab foundation

3 1/8" × 13 1/2" beam

2 × 4 framing 16" O.C.

2 × 4 pressure-treated mudsill

Materials List

- Pea gravel and concrete for slab foundation
- Rebar #4
- Pressure-treated mudsills 2 × 4
- Plates, wall/cripple studs, trimmer studs, and sills 2 × 4
- Window header 2 × 4
- Beam for overhead door header 3 1/8" × 13 1/2"
- OSB wall sheathing 7/16"
- CDX roof sheathing 1/2"
- Preengineered trusses with 4-in-12 slope
- Hip, common, and jack rafters 2 × 4
- Vapor retarder
- Lap siding 1/2" × 6"
- Prehung door 3'0" × 6'8"

- Sliding window 5'0" × 3'0"
- Cedar door wrap 2 × 6
- Cedar fascia 1 × 6
- Cedar corner and window wrap 1 × 4
- Cedar window trim 1 × 3
- Overhead door 16' × 8'
- Asphalt shingles and ridge caps
- Drip edge and 15-lb. roofing felt
- Anchor bolts
- Metal framing connectors
- Galvanized nails and outdoor screws
- Doorset
- Paint, stain, or water sealer

How to Build the Two-car Hip-roof Garage

This project begins with a sizable concrete slab (pages 66–67). You may wish to have a professional do that part. Once it's poured, the walls are straightforward to build, though the garage-door header will take some muscle to move. The roof framing is the challenge here, but it's simplified with the use of two types of preengineered trusses. Sheathing, siding, roofing, and trim are easy to install, but there's a lot of each one. In short, it's best to have some building experience and some strong helpers on hand.

1 **POUR THE SLAB.** First excavate for the slab foundation, install #4 rebar around the perimeter trench, and build forms. Add a layer of pea gravel or crushed stone; pour the concrete. Level and smooth the concrete, locate anchor positions for the mudsills, and install anchors in the still-wet concrete. Cure by misting the slab with water, covering it with plastic sheets, and keeping it damp for two to three days.

2 **FRAME THE WALLS.** First cut 2 by 4 pressure-treated mudsills for the perimeter. Transfer anchor locations and drill holes for the bolts to pass through. Cut top plates to match the mudsills, and lay out wall studs 16 inches on cen-

ter on both. Also lay out rough openings for the window, a side door, and the overhead door. (Note: The overhead door's rough opening is $1\frac{1}{2}$ inches higher and 3 inches wider than normal to allow for the addition of 2 by 6 cedar door wrap around the interior.) Cut sufficient studs to length (96 inches) and build the walls in sections. Add trimmer studs, headers, cripple studs, and sills as required.

3 **RAISE THE WALLS.** Starting with the side walls, place each wall section over the anchor bolts, slip on washers, and thread on nuts; tighten only hand-tight. Brace each wall as necessary and continue until all four walls are

continued ▶▶

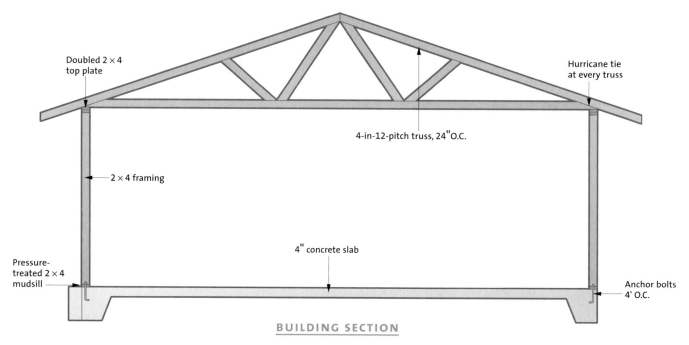

Doubled 2 × 4 top plate

Hurricane tie at every truss

4-in-12-pitch truss, 24" O.C.

2 × 4 framing

4" concrete slab

Pressure-treated 2 × 4 mudsill

Anchor bolts 4' O.C.

BUILDING SECTION

Two-car Reverse-gable Garage

Far from the typical cookie-cutter two-car garage, this structure illustrates the advantage of building up instead of out, preserving valuable yard space. The second floor of the garage can serve as a workshop or storage loft or both. An optional dormer brings in lots of natural light.

A "reverse-gable" garage is identical to a standard gable structure with one important difference: Instead of the garage door being located in one of the gabled ends, it's installed under the eaves on one of the long walls. This two-story garage rests on a slab foundation. Stairs inside lead to the second floor.

Laminated veneer lumber (LVL) is used for headers and for the single long beam that supports the second-story floor joists running the width of the garage. As an alternative to the long beam, you could run 14-inch I-joists (another engineered wood product) from the front plates to the back instead.

This is a challenging project for advanced carpenters only. The heavy beams and substantial heights call for extra skill, caution, and stamina. You may wish to farm out the framing, then do the finish work yourself.

DESIGN: W. ALEX TEIPEL, ARCHITECTURAL RESOURCES

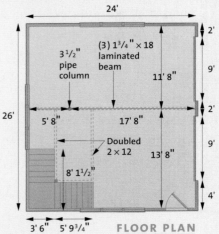

FLOOR PLAN

- 24'
- 2'
- 3½" pipe column
- (3) 1¾" × 18 laminated beam
- 11' 8"
- 9'
- 26'
- 2'
- 5' 8"
- 17' 8"
- Doubled 2 × 12
- 13' 8"
- 9'
- 8' 1½"
- 4'
- 3' 6"
- 5' 9¾"

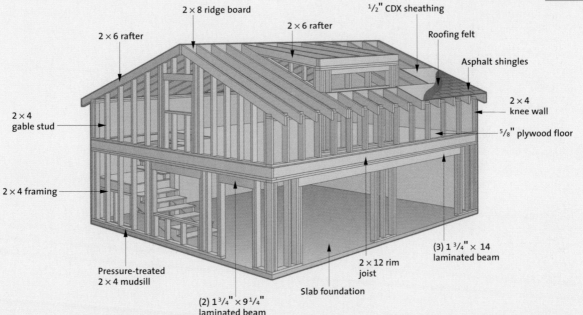

- 2 × 8 ridge board
- 2 × 6 rafter
- 2 × 6 rafter
- ½" CDX sheathing
- Roofing felt
- Asphalt shingles
- 2 × 4 gable stud
- 2 × 4 knee wall
- ⅝" plywood floor
- 2 × 4 framing
- (3) 1¾" × 14 laminated beam
- Pressure-treated 2 × 4 mudsill
- 2 × 12 rim joist
- Slab foundation
- (2) 1¾" × 9¼" laminated beam

up. Check for square, level, and plumb. Then screw the walls together at the corners and fully tighten the nuts on the mudsills. Next, cut double top plates, mark the truss locations every 24 inches on center on the two long ones, and install.

4 **FRAME THE ROOF.** Roof framing is simplified with the use of preengineered trusses (see the roof framing detail below). There are seven common trusses and three "stepped" trusses on each side of these. Start by attaching the center common truss to the double top plates, using rafter ties. Brace as needed. Then add the remaining trusses 24 inches on center, working toward the ends. Cut and attach hip rafters to the high point of the end stepped trusses; attach the loose ends of the hip rafters to the double top plates with rafter ties. Finally, cut and attach common and jack rafters at each end.

5 **APPLY THE ROOFING.** Cover the roof framing with ½-inch CDX plywood, then add drip edge and 15-pound roofing felt. Cover it with asphalt shingles and install the ridge caps.

6 **ADD THE SIDING.** To enclose the walls, start by cutting and installing sheathing. Cover this with a vapor retarder and install the sliding window and prehung door. Then cut and attach the 6-inch lap siding.

7 **APPLY THE TRIM.** Cut and install the 1 by 6 cedar fascia, 1 by 4 cedar corner boards and window wrap, and 1 by 3 cedar window trim. Nail the 2 by 6 cedar door wrap around the top and side edges of the garage door opening. Install the overhead door or have it installed professionally.

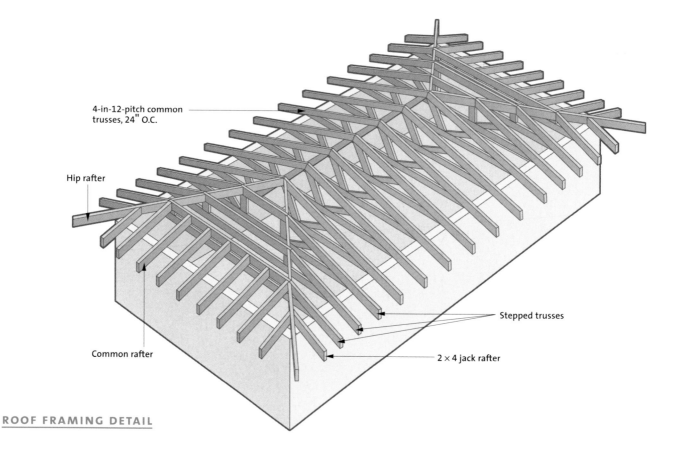

4-in-12-pitch common trusses, 24" O.C.

Hip rafter

Common rafter

Stepped trusses

2 × 4 jack rafter

ROOF FRAMING DETAIL

Two-car Gable with Summer Room

DESIGN: W. ALEX TEIPEL, ARCHITECTURAL RESOURCES

Space and grace combine in this generous 24- by 38-foot garage designed for two cars. The attached summer room boasts windows on three sides, a half-bath, and even a fireplace. Because the room's ceiling is open to the rafters, it seems even bigger—and better.

The place where two rooflines meet is called a valley. Valleys are typically supported by a valley rafter that extends from the outside wall of the extended area to the ridge board or header. Because these valley rafters support considerable weight under snow load, they should be engineered for your locale.

Consider hiring a pro to frame the roof. You'll also want to hire a mason to build the fireplace box and chimney. The interior of the summer room can be insulated and finished with drywall; in temperate climates, you might decide to leave the studs bare for a true summer-cottage effect.

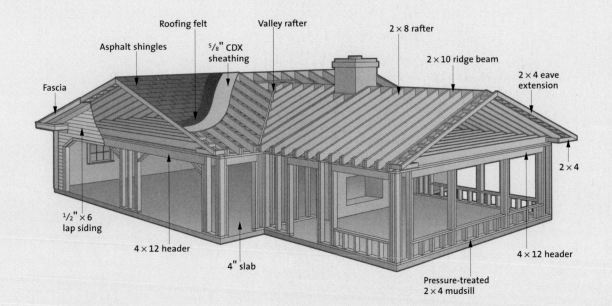

Roofing felt
Valley rafter
2 × 8 rafter
Asphalt shingles
⁵⁄₈" CDX sheathing
2 × 10 ridge beam
2 × 4 eave extension
Fascia
2 × 4
¹⁄₂" × 6 lap siding
4 × 12 header
4" slab
4 × 12 header
Pressure-treated 2 × 4 mudsill

GAMBREL MINIBARN

FOR SERIOUS STORAGE and lots of headroom, consider this gambrel-roof shed. The 12- by 16-foot minibarn has a ramp and generous double doors that make the ins and outs of storage easy. Planks laid across the collar ties can add even more usable space overhead.

Design Details

Reminiscent of a timber-framed barn, this scaled-down version uses many of the same construction principles. The 4 by 6 corner posts team up with 4 by 4 top plates and door posts, plus 2 by 4 middle rails, to form stout wall frames. Studs

DESIGN: KEVIN DOWN, NORTHERN PINE SHEDS

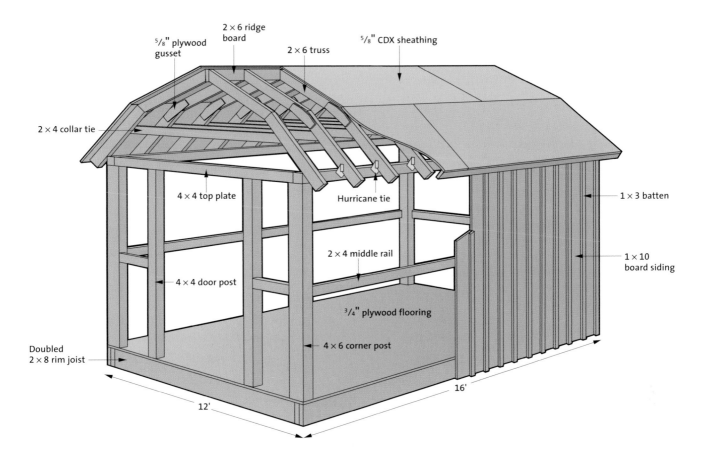

2 × 6 ridge board

⁵/₈" plywood gusset

2 × 6 truss

⁵/₈" CDX sheathing

2 × 4 collar tie

4 × 4 top plate

Hurricane tie

1 × 3 batten

2 × 4 middle rail

1 × 10 board siding

4 × 4 door post

³/₄" plywood flooring

Doubled 2 × 8 rim joist

4 × 6 corner post

16'

12'

aren't required, since the board-and-batten siding (attached to the top plate, middle rail, and framed floor) helps bear the weight of the roof. If you wish, you can safely substitute pairs of 2 by 4s nailed together every 6 inches or so for the 4 by 4s.

The gambrel roof is framed by making rafterlike truss sections that attach to the ridge board. Collar ties span the truss sections for extra strength. If desired, you can place windows above the middle rail by cutting openings in the siding and attaching flanged windows.

Materials List

• Concrete and pea gravel for footings	
• Pressure-treated floor joists	2 × 8
• Tongue-and-groove plywood flooring	³/₄"
• Corner posts	4 × 6
• Top plates and door posts	4 × 4
• Middle rails and collar ties	2 × 4
• Rough-sawn siding	1 × 10
• Corner and door trim, siding battens	1 × 3
• Rafters/trusses	2 × 6
• Ridge board	2 × 6
• CDX roof sheathing and gussets	⁵/₈"
• Fascia	1 × 6
• Drip edge and 15-lb. roofing felt	
• Asphalt shingles and ridge caps	
• Galvanized nails and outdoor screws	
• Metal framing brackets and fasteners	
• Strap hinges and door latch	
• Paint, stain, or water sealer	

How to Build the Gambrel Minibarn

The size and weight of this structure require poured footings (page 63) or a reinforced concrete slab. If you choose a slab, you won't need to build the framed floor described in Step 1 below—but you will need to add mudsills at the bottom of each wall to nail the siding to. Be sure to have at least one strong helper on hand to handle the heavy 4 by 4s and 4 by 6s. If you're not great at toenailing (page 71), consider making these post-and-beam connections with metal framing connectors (page 47).

1 **FRAME THE FLOOR.** The outside rim joists for the floor are made from doubled pressure-treated 2 by 8s. The side pieces are 16 feet long and the end joists are 11 feet 6 inches, to make a 12- by 16-foot floor frame. Join the outside frame pieces with 16d nails and L-brackets on the inside corners. Set this frame on the footings, square it up, and secure it to the footings with metal post anchors. For the internal joists, cut pressure-treated 2 by 8s to 11 feet 6 inches and attach them to the frame with joist hangers, 24 inches on center. Cover the completed frame with ¾-inch tongue-and-groove plywood, using 8d nails or 2-inch galvanized deck screws.

2 **BUILD THE FRONT AND BACK WALLS.** Cut four 4 by 6 corner posts 7 feet long for the front and rear walls. Cut two top plates 11 feet 5 inches long to rest on the corner posts, leaving 3½ inches free for the top plate of each side wall. Mark positions for the door posts according to the width of door you want. Lay the top plates and posts for the front wall on the floor and connect them by toenailing 16d nails or using metal framing connectors. Build the rear wall in the same manner.

With a helper, tip the front and back walls into position and attach the posts to the floor with 16d galvanized nails or metal framing connectors.

3 **LEVEL AND PLUMB THE WALLS.** Check the walls for level and plumb and add temporary diagonal bracing inside the shed from post to post to keep each square. To hold the walls upright and plumb, add 4-foot-long vertical braces reaching from the floor framing to midway up each corner post. Cut and attach the 2 by 4 middle rails 36 inches up from the floor. Recheck each wall for plumb.

4 **ADD THE SIDE TOP PLATES.** Next cut the side top plates to 16 feet, or long enough to overlap the top of each 4 by 6 corner post. Clamp or tack the top plates together, and mark the rafter locations 24 inches on center; mark their locations on the 2 by 6 ridge board as well. Attach the top plates. Also add the middle rails between the posts. Attach temporary 1 by 4 diagonal braces to the inside of the walls to keep them from racking. Recheck the entire structure for plumb and level and adjust as necessary.

5 **ADD THE SIDING.** Begin filling in the wall frames by cutting 1 by 10 siding boards to 93½ inches for the long eave sides and attaching them flush with the top plate.

6 **INSTALL THE GABLE BOARDS.** Next, cut 1 by 10 siding boards 12 feet long for the gable walls and install them so they run long on top (they will be trimmed to length after the rafters are up).

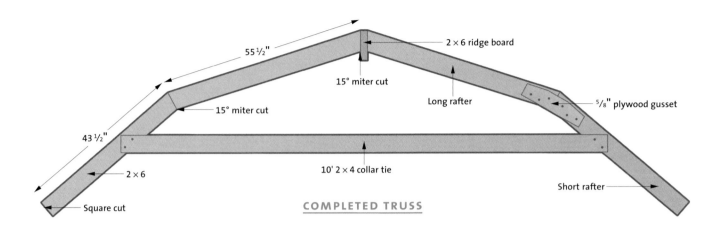

55½"

2 × 6 ridge board

15° miter cut

Long rafter

⅝" plywood gusset

15° miter cut

43½"

10' 2 × 4 collar tie

2 × 6

Short rafter

Square cut

COMPLETED TRUSS

7 **FRAME THE ROOF.** Start the roof by temporarily tacking the ridge board to the gable siding so it's centered 11 feet 6 inches up from the floor. Then cut pairs of short and long rafters as shown above. Make a truss section assembly jig (shown below) and then fabricate each side of the truss by attaching ⅝-inch plywood gussets to the pairs of rafters, using 8d nails or 2-inch screws.

8 **CUT THE GABLE ENDS.** Hold a truss section up against the inside of the gable siding and ridge board and mark the outline on the siding; cut to the marked line with a circular saw or reciprocating saw and repeat for the opposite end. Attach the end trusses to the ridge board, top plate, and siding. Nail the remaining rafter pairs to the ridge

board and secure them to the top plates with metal fasteners known as hurricane ties. Connect the truss sections with 10-foot-long collar ties, using 16d nails. Then cut and attach 1 by 6 fascia to the ends of the rafters.

9 **FINISH THE ROOF.** Cover the roof frame with ⅝-inch CDX plywood sheathing, starting at the bottom and working up toward the ridge. Add drip edge and 15-pound roofing felt. Install asphalt shingles and ridge caps.

10 **ADD THE DOOR AND TRIM.** First, cut and attach 1 by 3 corner trim and door trim. Then cover the siding seams with 1 by 3 battens cut to the same length. Build a pair of doors to fit the opening (see the detail drawing on page 116). Attach the doors to the frame with strap hinges and add a door latch.

If desired, install screening between the ends of the rafters and the top plates to keep out insects. If you'd like to build a ramp like the one shown, see page 94.

⅝" CDX plywood base (to be used later for roof sheathing)

Long rafter

1 × 2 cleat screwed to base

⅝" plywood gusset

Short rafter

TRUSS SECTION ASSEMBLY JIG

Compact Sheep Barn

This full-fledged barn sits on a trim, 18- by 24-foot footprint. Essentially, the design joins a central gable structure with a shed-roof annex that shelters sheep. An upstairs loft holds feed; it's accessed via the loft door in front and a framed floor opening in back.

The sheep barn uses post-and-beam Douglas fir framing; the heavy members are notched and bolted together. The easiest way to cut the notches is with a circular saw and a chisel—for details, see page 110. Short diagonal braces help keep things square; horizontal rails add extra support and a nailing surface for the vertical siding boards. The central wall can be left open or covered—in this barn, there's a short partition that divides the main space from the sheep pen. If you leave the wall open, you may wish to replace the mudsill there with post anchors so the floor is open, too. Or just frame in a doorway.

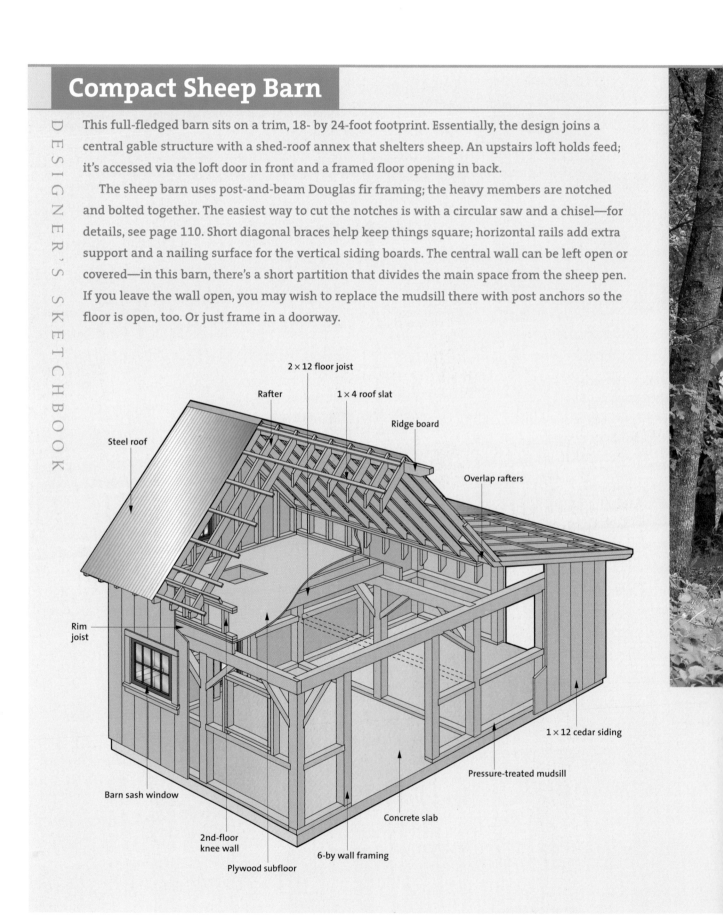

2 × 12 floor joist

Rafter

1 × 4 roof slat

Ridge board

Steel roof

Overlap rafters

Rim joist

1 × 12 cedar siding

Pressure-treated mudsill

Barn sash window

2nd-floor knee wall

Concrete slab

6-by wall framing

Plywood subfloor

DESIGN: ROBERT GIOMI AND MICHAEL KATZ

Joists for the second-floor loft are 2 by 12 fir; a plywood subfloor and short knee walls sit atop the joists, and the main rafters rest on these. The rafters for the shed roof overlap the main rafters atop the inside knee wall.

Striking 1 by 12 cedar siding was nailed to the post-and-beam walls, and a corrugated steel roof sits on 1 by 4 slats atop the rafters. Recycled barn sash windows fit in cedar frames. Finishing touches include sliding batten doors in front, the hayloft door above, and another outdoor slider to the sheep pen that's paneled with open wire mesh.

SMALL GABLE BARN

COUNTRY CHARM AND COLONIAL STYLE MERGE in this smallish barn that's big on flexibility. Use the entire 10- by 16-foot interior for storage or divvy it up for storage plus playroom (or office or workshop). This design sports double doors both on the front and on one gable end for ready access. (To buy this shed in kit form, see page 159.)

Design Details

Despite the custom touches, this 2 by 4 stick-framed barn is relatively easy to build. The roofing is simplified with 2 by 4 trusses that you make on-site. The siding is T1-11 plywood, which goes on quickly.

DESIGN: BETTER BARNS

10-in-12-pitch trusses, 24" O.C.

1 × 2 fascia

1 × 4 fascia

½" CDX sheathing

Roofing felt

Asphalt shingles

Opening for transom windows

1 × 4 trim

Concrete block

T1–11 exterior siding

Pressure-treated 2 × 6 floor joist

Site-built doors

¾" plywood flooring

Pressure-treated 2 × 8 mudsill

Like many gable-roofed structures, this barn is stretchable. If you need a wider entryway or more interior space, simply alter the plan and lengthen the barn. This design includes a row of transom windows above the gable-end doors—a great way to enhance interior illumination.

The barn described here is built on concrete blocks atop a pea-gravel base. Make sure to ask your local building inspector if this is allowed in your area. If you need to use poured footings, see page 65.

Materials List

• Pea gravel and concrete blocks or piers for foundation	
• Concrete patio blocks as needed to level	
• Pressure-treated mudsills	2 × 8
• Pressure-treated floor framing	2 × 6
• Tongue-and-groove plywood flooring	¾"
• Plates, studs, headers, cripple studs, trimmer studs, sills, trusses, subfascia	2 × 4
• CDX roof sheathing and gussets	½"
• T1-11 exterior siding	⅝"
• Cedar fascia	1 × 2, 1 × 4
• Corner, window, and door trim	1 × 4
• Drip edge and 15-lb. roofing felt	
• Asphalt shingles and ridge caps	
• Barn sash windows	3'0" × 2'0"
• Tongue-and-groove cedar for door and door bracing	1 × 6
• Galvanized nails and deck screws	
• Strap hinges and door latch	
• Paint or stain	

How to Build the Gable Barn

This project breaks down into four easy pieces: block foundation, stick-framed walls, truss-formed roof, and finish work. Once you've got the floor for this small barn framed and covered, it's convenient to fabricate the roof trusses so you can use the floor as workspace before the walls are erected.

1 INSTALL THE FOUNDATION. Start by leveling an 11- by 17-foot rectangle. Excavate 4 inches of soil and replace it with pea gravel for drainage. Then place twelve 4- by 8- by 16-inch concrete blocks in three rows spaced 59 inches apart running the long dimension. Find the high point and shim the lower blocks level, using additional blocks or thinner patio pavers. (For more on block foundations, see page 62.)

2 BUILD THE FLOOR. The floor is framed with pressure-treated 2 by 6 lumber and attaches to 16-foot-long 2 by 8 mudsills that rest on the concrete blocks. To begin, nail together a 2 by 6 rim joist and a 2 by 8 mudsill for the front and another pair for the back (see the foundation detail below); cut a third mudsill to fit on top of the center blocks. Then lay out floor joists 16 inches on center. Place mudsills on top of the blocks, then cut 2 by 6 joists to a length of 9 feet 9 inches and insert them between rim joists; secure with 16d nails or joist hangers. Top the floor frame with ³⁄₄-inch tongue-and-groove plywood, and secure it with 8d galvanized nails.

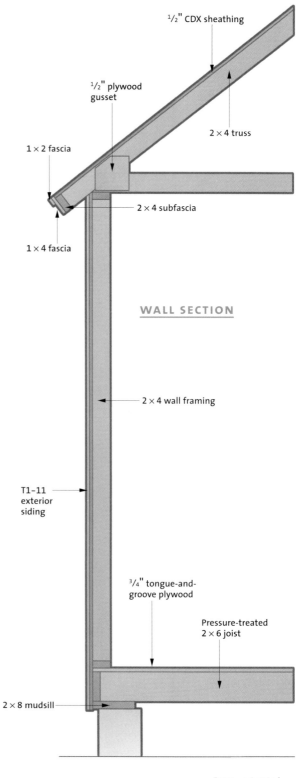

½" CDX sheathing

½" plywood gusset

1 × 2 fascia

2 × 4 truss

2 × 4 subfascia

1 × 4 fascia

WALL SECTION

2 × 4 wall framing

T1–11 exterior siding

³⁄₄" tongue-and-groove plywood

Pressure-treated 2 × 6 joist

2 × 8 mudsill

FOUNDATION DETAIL

Pressure-treated 2 × 6 rim joist

Concrete block

Pressure-treated 2 × 6 joist

Pressure-treated 2 × 8 mudsill

3 **ASSEMBLE ROOF TRUSSES.** Each truss is made up of two 2 by 4 rafters and one 2 by 4 cross brace joined together with plywood gussets (see the roof framing detail below). The easiest way to build these is to lay out rafters on the barn floor and build the trusses there. Cut the rafters to length with a 40-degree angle cut at one end. Also cut the gussets and cross braces to size. Note that the gable-end trusses have an extra cross brace to serve as a nailer for the gable siding.

4 **BUILD THE WALLS.** Start by cutting the top and bottom plates: For the front and back walls, cut them 16 feet long; for the sides, cut them 9 feet 5 inches. Working with one wall at a time, lay out the studs on the floor every 16 inches on center and locate rough openings. The front window openings are $14 \frac{1}{2}$ inches in from the wall ends, $36 \frac{1}{4}$ inches wide, and $25 \frac{1}{4}$ inches high; the bottom of each header is 72 inches up from the floor. The 58- by 72-inch doors are centered on both the front and left-hand walls. Place studs between the top and bottom plates and secure with 16d nails; add headers, trimmers, sills, and cripple studs as needed.

5 **RAISE THE WALLS.** Lift each wall into position and secure it to the floor with 3-inch deck screws; brace as needed (page 73). When the walls are square, level, and plumb, screw the corners of the walls together. If you're planning on adding an internal partition wall (shown on page 147), also frame and install it at this point.

6 **INSTALL THE ROOF.** First cut and attach T1-11 plywood siding to the gable-end trusses you built earlier, then attach these to the top plates of the gable-end walls, securing them with 3-inch screws. Install the remaining trusses, one over each pair of wall studs, bracing them as needed. Attach 2 by 4 subfascia to the truss ends as shown in the wall section at left. Then add both 1 by 4 and 1 by 2 fascia atop the subfascia and along the gable ends. Sheath the roof with $\frac{1}{2}$-inch CDX plywood. Install 15-pound roofing felt, add drip edge, and install asphalt shingles and ridge caps. (See pages 78–79 for more on roofing techniques.)

continued ▶▶

ROOF FRAMING DETAIL

$\frac{1}{2}$" plywood gusset

10-in-12 pitch

87"

$\frac{1}{2}$" plywood gusset

Extra 2 × 4 crosspiece for gable-end trusses

Truss shoe

120"

$\frac{1}{2}$" plywood gusset

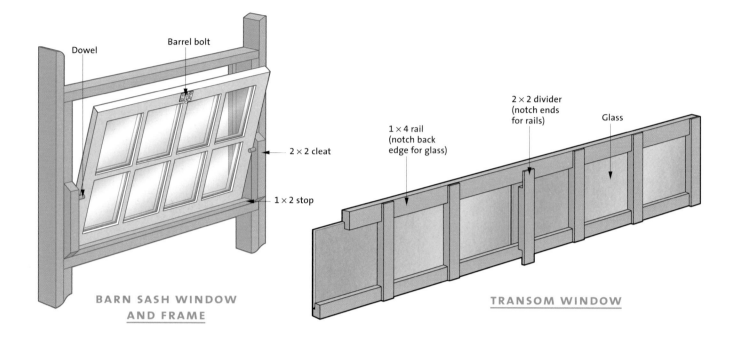

BARN SASH WINDOW AND FRAME

Dowel

Barrel bolt

2 × 2 cleat

1 × 2 stop

TRANSOM WINDOW

1 × 4 rail (notch back edge for glass)

2 × 2 divider (notch ends for rails)

Glass

7 **COVER THE WALLS.** Enclose the wall areas with T1-11 siding, securing it with 8d nails every 8 inches or so. Install trim around the window and door openings and at the corners of the barn to cover the exposed siding edges.

8 **ADD DOORS AND WINDOWS.** Use 2- by 3-foot barn sash windows and make simple frames to accept them, as shown at top left; the windows are held closed at the top with a barrel bolt.

The transom window is a 5-foot-long ladder frame (top right) backed by a single pane of glass or, if you prefer, a pair of shorter panes as shown. The two panes are easier to handle than one longer piece; hide the seam behind one of the vertical 2 by 2s.

The doors are built from 1 by 6 tongue-and-groove cedar and Z-bracing cut from 1-by stock; attach the braces with $1\frac{1}{4}$-inch screws, and hang doors with heavy-duty strap hinges. Finally, add a latch.

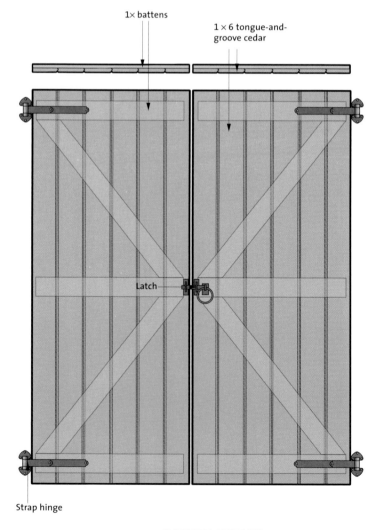

1× battens

1 × 6 tongue-and-groove cedar

Latch

Strap hinge

BATTEN DOORS

Red Gable Barn

This handsome Colonial minibarn, which graces our book cover, is a variation on the small gable barn shown on page 146. Like its cousin, this slightly larger 12- by 16-foot structure sits atop a concrete block foundation with 2 by 8 mudsills, 2 by 6 floor joists, and 2 by 4 walls; the roof is framed from site-made trusses.

Unlike the gable barn, this one is sided with vertical tongue-and-groove pine boards, and if that's

DESIGN: BETTER BARNS

your choice, you need horizontal blocking to nail them to. Here, the blocking is continuous 2 by 4 rails notched into the studs in post-and-beam fashion (the simplest way to do this is with a circular saw and chisel, as shown on page 110). You could also simply use short 2 by 4 blocks nailed between studs (page 83). To purchase plans or to buy this shed in kit form, see page 159.

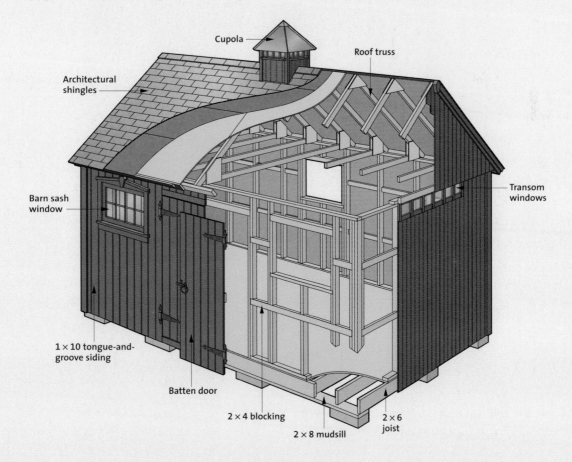

Cupola

Roof truss

Architectural shingles

Transom windows

Barn sash window

1 × 10 tongue-and-groove siding

Batten door

2 × 4 blocking

2 × 8 mudsill

2 × 6 joist

Horse Barn

Corral some serious space with this handsome, sturdy horse barn that adapts to multiple needs. At 30 feet by 50 feet, it accommodates eight horse stalls, a hayloft, and accessory rooms. Or use it as the ultimate workshop. This is a major project—you may want to hire pros for most of the structure and complete the detailing yourself.

Professional barn builders prefabricate as much of a barn as possible and then assemble it on site. You could use a similar technique by building the long walls first, gathering your friends for a barn-raising, and erecting the walls atop concrete footings. Next, connect the two sections with ceiling joists, add a floor, and frame the roof. Then fill the ground-floor section between the stalls with concrete and cover the openings at each end with sliding doors.

The strength of this structure comes from the heavy beams and the board-and-batten siding. Don't use other siding without reengineering the framing. Also, oak must be used for the frame pieces; pine and fir are not strong enough.

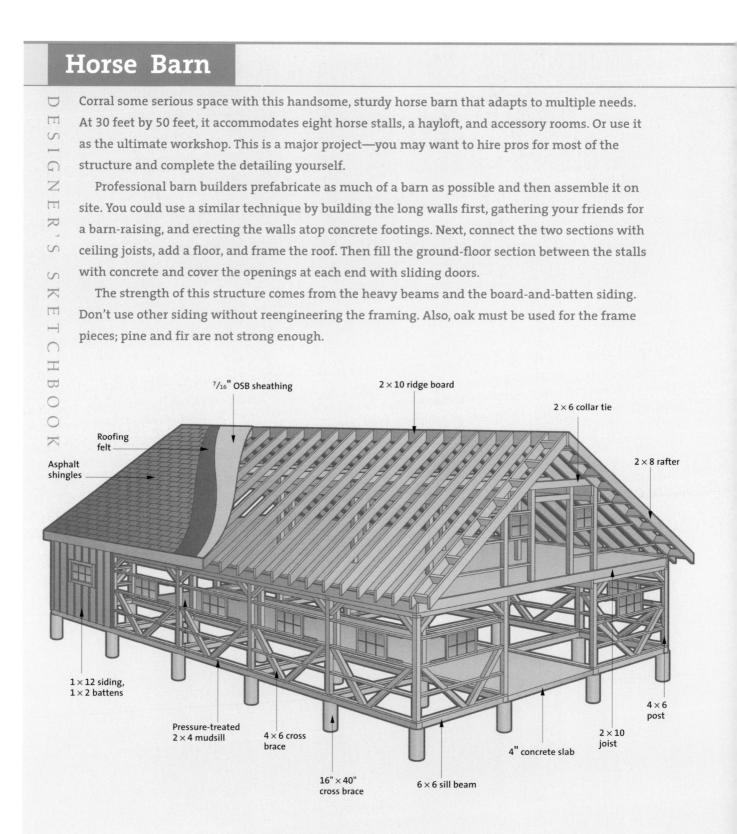

7/16" OSB sheathing

2 × 10 ridge board

2 × 6 collar tie

Roofing felt

2 × 8 rafter

Asphalt shingles

1 × 12 siding, 1 × 2 battens

Pressure-treated 2 × 4 mudsill

4 × 6 cross brace

16" × 40" cross brace

6 × 6 sill beam

4" concrete slab

2 × 10 joist

4 × 6 post

DESIGN: GROFFDALE BARNS

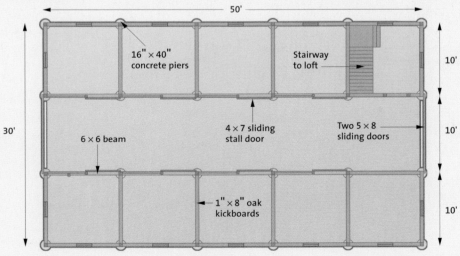

50'

16" × 40"
concrete piers

Stairway
to loft

10'

30'

6 × 6 beam

4 × 7 sliding
stall door

Two 5 × 8
sliding doors

10'

1" × 8" oak
kickboards

10'

FLOOR PLAN

INTERIOR OPTIONS

NO MATTER HOW LARGE or small your new shed, garage, or barn, you'll probably want to maximize the storage space inside. You may also be outfitting a spot to pursue a hobby or craft. Either way, here are some projects that will spruce up your new structure.

Hooks, Racks, and Shelves

Hanging hooks and wall organizers are readily available; for a sampling, see page 35. But you can also make your own. Hooks slotted in pegboard are the old standby. Or you can simply run a 1 by 4 rail across wall studs and add assorted hooks from the home center.

It's easy to build recessed shelving by first gluing and screwing short cleats to open wall studs. Then you cut shelves to fit between the studs and screw them to the cleats. Or notch shelves as shown at left. Tracks and brackets are even easier; for sheds and garages, look for the heavy-duty, two-prong type shown below. Screw the tracks to wall studs, mount the brackets, and add shelves: For the strongest spans, make them from ¾-inch plywood and 1 by 2 lips, or even two layers of plywood glued together (see facing page).

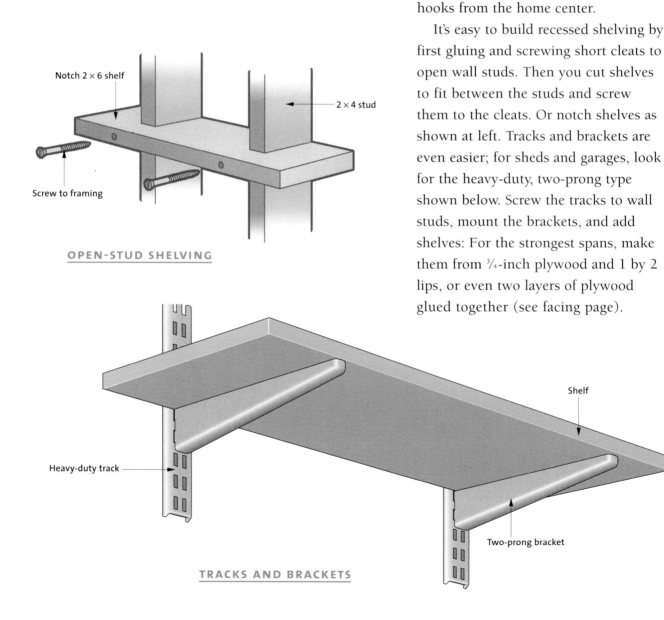

Notch 2 × 6 shelf

2 × 4 stud

Screw to framing

OPEN-STUD SHELVING

Heavy-duty track

Shelf

Two-prong bracket

TRACKS AND BRACKETS

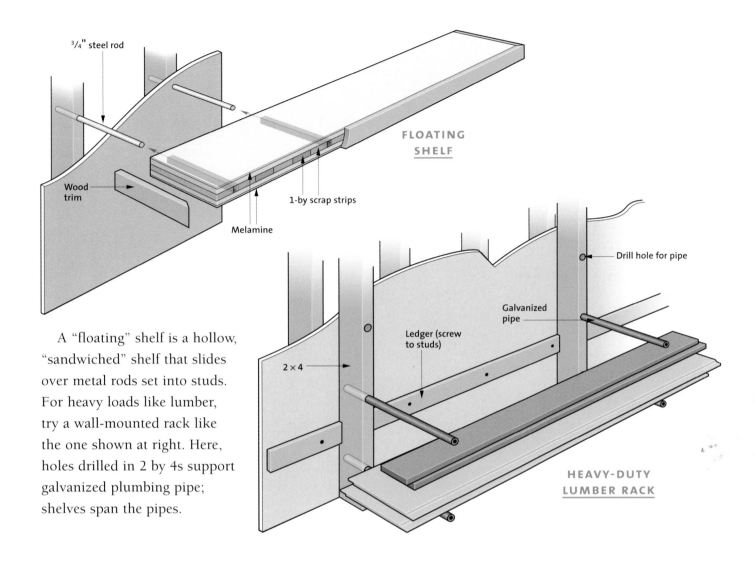

³/₄" steel rod

FLOATING SHELF

Wood trim

Melamine

1-by scrap strips

Drill hole for pipe

Galvanized pipe

Ledger (screw to studs)

2 × 4

HEAVY-DUTY LUMBER RACK

A "floating" shelf is a hollow, "sandwiched" shelf that slides over metal rods set into studs. For heavy loads like lumber, try a wall-mounted rack like the one shown at right. Here, holes drilled in 2 by 4s support galvanized plumbing pipe; shelves span the pipes.

PLYWOOD SHELVES

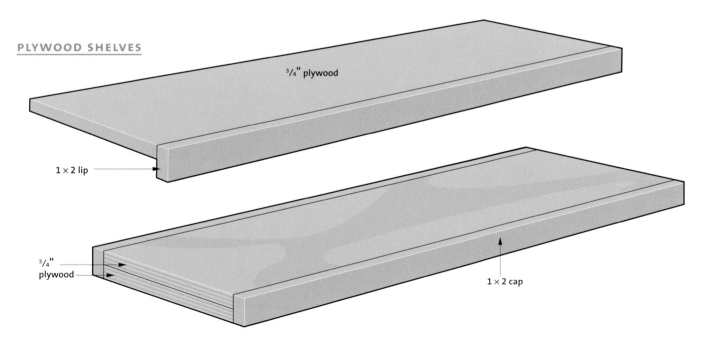

³/₄" plywood

1 × 2 lip

³/₄" plywood

1 × 2 cap

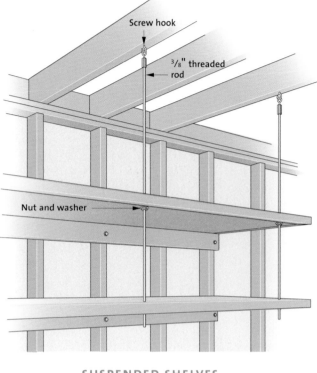

SUSPENDED SHELVES

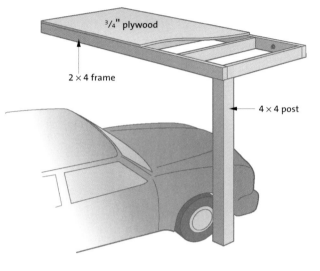

OVER-CAR PLATFORM

Overhead Options

Out of wall space? Look up! Make the most of the area where ceiling meets walls by hanging shelves from suspended 2-by hangers. Or use threaded metal rods instead, as shown above.

In a garage, create storage space above parked cars by building a platform made from a 2 by 4 frame and plywood. Try using existing ceiling joists or collar ties—or new ones you add for the purpose—to effectively build a "loft." You can even add a ladder or pull-down stairs.

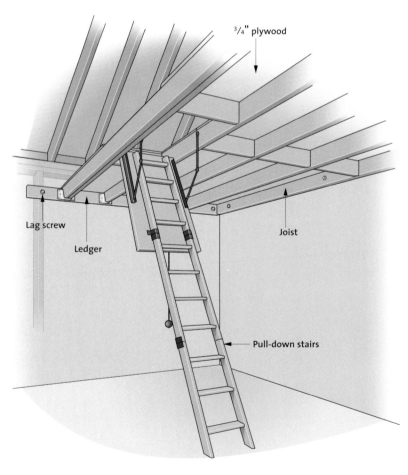

OVERHEAD LOFT

Benches and Built-ins

Potting sheds and greenhouses call for some serious counter space. Basic plant benches are easy to make by building frames from 2 by 4s and covering them with spaced boards, exterior plywood, or even hollow-core doors.

Or maybe you'd prefer a trim, built-in bench. If so, simply support the back on a ledger and the front on legs. Or go "legs-free" entirely with gussets or homemade brackets screwed to open wall studs—as shown below. *continued* ▶▶

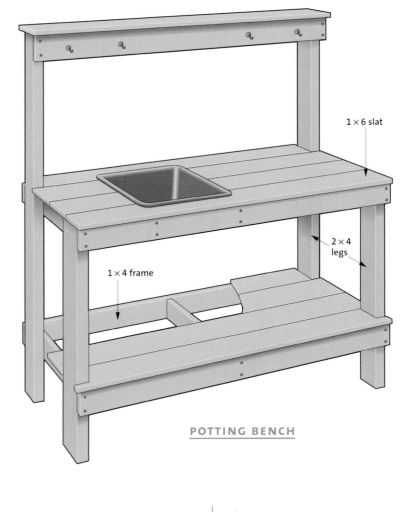

1 × 6 slat

2 × 4 legs

1 × 4 frame

POTTING BENCH

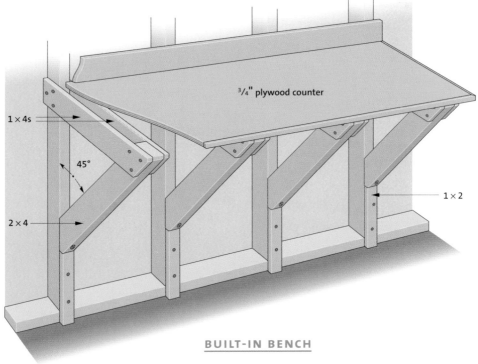

3/4" plywood counter

1 × 4s

45°

2 × 4

1 × 2

BUILT-IN BENCH

CRAFTS TABLE

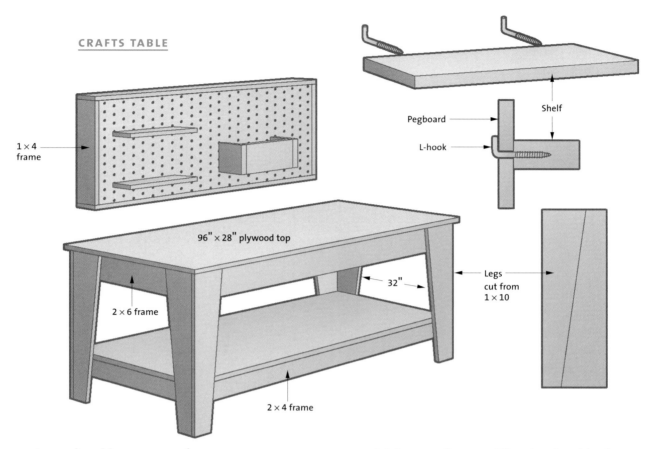

1 × 4 frame

Pegboard

Shelf

L-hook

96" × 28" plywood top

2 × 6 frame

32"

Legs cut from 1 × 10

2 × 4 frame

A sturdy table or two and some storage space are essential for a crafts area. The simple table shown above consists of a 2-by frame, legs cut from 1 by 10s, and a top made from plywood. To create a tougher top surface that won't stain, attach a layer of plastic laminate with contact cement.

A workbench is usually the command center. A classic hardwood version is shown below. An easy-to-build softwood bench is shown on the facing page.

HARDWOOD WORKBENCH

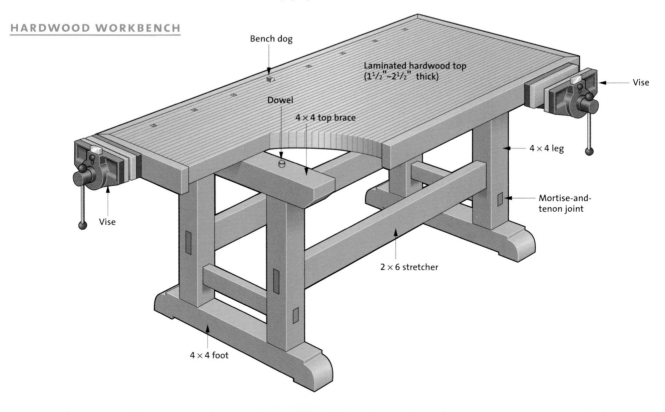

Bench dog

Laminated hardwood top ($1\frac{1}{2}$"–$2\frac{1}{2}$" thick)

Vise

Dowel

4 × 4 top brace

4 × 4 leg

Mortise-and-tenon joint

Vise

2 × 6 stretcher

4 × 4 foot

BASIC SOFTWOOD WORKBENCH

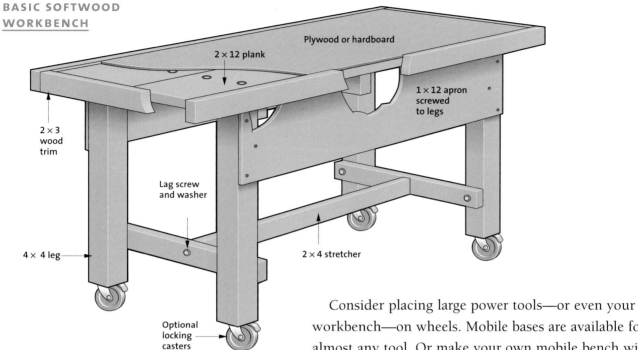

Plywood or hardboard

2 × 12 plank

1 × 12 apron screwed to legs

2 × 3 wood trim

Lag screw and washer

4 × 4 leg

2 × 4 stretcher

Optional locking casters

Consider placing large power tools—or even your workbench—on wheels. Mobile bases are available for almost any tool. Or make your own mobile bench with a set of locking casters and a layer or two of sturdy plywood. When not in use, both bench and tools can be rolled up against the walls or back into a corner.

Resources

Architectural Resources
W. Alex Teipel
(630) 232-1774 (Illinois)

Better Barns
(203) 266-7989 (Connecticut)
www.betterbarns.com

Cedarshed Industries, Inc.
(800) 830-8033 (British Columbia)
www.cedarshed.com

Garages, Etc.
(800) 287-3910 (Washington)
www.garagesetcinc.com

Garlinghouse Company
(800) 235-5700 (Virginia)
www.garlinghouse.com

Groffdale Barns
(717) 687-8350 (Pennsylvania)
www.groffdalebarns.com

Modern-Shed
(206) 524-1188 (Washington)
www.modern-shed.com

Summerwood Products
(866) 519-4634 (Ontario)
www.summerwood.com

Walpole Woodworkers
(800) 343-6948 (Massachusetts)
www.walpolewoodworkers.com

SHED AND GARAGE PLANS

A NEW GARAGE OR SHED CAN SOLVE YOUR STORAGE PROBLEMS, provide a protected area for your car, and add charm to your property. If the projects featured earlier in this book weren't quite what you are looking for, or if you need more detailed building plans, then check out the plans for sale on the following pages. Whether you need a simple shed to house your garden tools or an elaborate garage that extends your living space, you'll find a wide variety of options. And if you build it yourself, you'll have the added satisfaction of watching the structure take shape with each saw cut and swing of the hammer. The opposite page provides all the ordering information you'll need. Just choose the plan that's right for you from the selection beginning on page 162 and call, fax, or mail in your order; you will be well on your way to an exciting new building project.

Important Information to Know Before you Order

• Exchange Policies—Since blueprints are printed in response to your order, we cannot honor requests for refunds. However, if for some reason you find that the plan you have purchased does not meet your requirements, you may exchange that plan for another plan in our collection. At the time of the exchange, you will be charged a processing fee of 25% of your original plan package price, plus the difference in price between the plan packages (if applicable) and the cost to ship the new plans to you.

Please note: Reproducible drawings can only be exchanged if the package is unopened, and exchanges are allowed only within 90 days of purchase.

• Building Codes & Requirements—At the time the construction drawings were prepared, every effort was made to ensure that these plans and specifications meet nationally recognized codes. Our plans conform to most national building codes. Because building codes vary from area to area, some drawing modifications and/or the assistance of a professional designer or architect may be necessary to comply with your local codes or to accommodate specific building site conditions. We advise you to consult with your local building official for information regarding codes governing your area.

HOW TO ORDER

For fastest service,
Call toll-free 1-800-367-7667 day or night

Three Easy Ways to Order

1. CALL toll free 1-800-367-7667 for credit card orders. MasterCard, Visa, Discover, and American Express are accepted.

2. FAX your order to 1-314-770-2226.

3. MAIL the Order Form to:
   HDA, Inc.
   944 Anglum Road
   St. Louis, MO 63042
   Attn: Customer Service Dept.

   QUESTIONS? Call Our Customer Service Number:
   1-800-367-7667

ORDER FORM

Please send me:

PLAN NUMBER 602-_____

PRICE CODE_____(see Plan Page)

Reproducible Masters (see chart at right) $ _____

Initial Set of Plans $ _____

Additional Plan Sets (see chart at right)
_____(Qty) at $_____each $ _____

Subtotal $ _____

Sales Tax (MO residents add 7%) $ _____

❑ Shipping/Handling (see chart at right) $ _____
(each additional set add $2.00 to shipping charges)

TOTAL ENCLOSED (US funds only) $ _____

❑ Enclosed is my check or money order payable to HDA, Inc. (Sorry, no COD's)

I hereby authorize HDA, Inc. to charge this purchase to my credit card account (check one):

❑ MasterCard ❑ VISA ❑ DISCOVER ❑ American Express Cards

Credit Card Number

Expiration Date

Signature

Name

Street Address   (Please print or type)

City   (Please do not use PO Box)

State   Zip

Daytime Phone Number (   ) -

Thank you for your order!

BLUEPRINT PRICE SCHEDULE

Price Code	1 Set	Additional Sets	Reproducible Masters
P4	$20.00	$10.00	$70.00
P5	$25.00	$10.00	$75.00
P6	$30.00	$10.00	$80.00
P7	$50.00	$10.00	$100.00
P8	$75.00	$10.00	$125.00
P9	$125.00	$20.00	$200.00
P10	$150.00	$20.00	$225.00
P11	$175.00	$20.00	$250.00
P12	$200.00	$20.00	$275.00
P13	$310.00	$45.00	$525.00

Plan prices are subject to change without notice.

Please note that plans are not refundable.

SHIPPING & HANDLING CHARGES

FOR EACH ADDITIONAL SET, ADD $2.00 TO SHIPPING CHARGES

U.S. SHIPPING

Regular (allow 7–10 business days)	$5.95
Priority (allow 3–5 business days)	$15.00
Express* (allow 1–2 business days)	$25.00

CANADA SHIPPING**

Standard (allow 8–12 business days)	$15.00
Express* (allow 3–5 business days)	$40.00

OVERSEAS SHIPPING/INTERNATIONAL

Call, fax, or e-mail (plans@hdainc.com) for shipping costs.

* For express delivery, please call us by 11:00 A.M. Monday–Friday CST

** Orders may be subject to custom's fees and/or duties/taxes

Design #602-002D-4500

SALT BOX
STORAGE SHEDS

- Sizes: 8' wide x 8' deep
- 12' wide x 8' deep
- 16' wide x 8' deep
- Wood floor on gravel base or concrete floor
- Height floor to peak: 8'-2"
- Front wall height: 7'-0"
- 6'-0" x 6'-5" double-door
- Complete list of materials
- Step-by-step instructions

Price Code P5

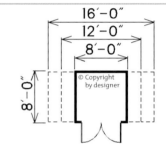

Design #602-002D-4502

YARD BARNS

- Sizes: 10' wide x 12' deep
- 10' wide x 16' deep
- 10' wide x 20' deep
- Wood floor on 4 x 4 runners
- Height floor to peak: 8'-4 $\frac{1}{2}$"
- Ceiling height: 6'-4"
- 4'-0" x 6'-4" double-door for easy access
- Complete list of materials
- Step-by-step instructions

Price Code P5

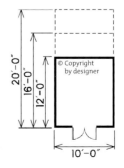

Design #602-002D-4501

BARN STORAGE SHEDS WITH LOFT

- Sizes: 12' wide x 12' deep
  - 12' wide x 16' deep
  - 12' wide x 20' deep
- Wood floor on concrete pier foundation or concrete floor
- Height floor to peak: 12'-10"
- Ceiling height: 7'-4"
- 4'-0" x 6'-8" double-door
- Complete list of materials
- Step-by-step instructions

Price Code P5

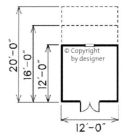

Design #602-002D-4515

GARDEN SHEDS WITH CLERESTORY

- Sizes: 10' wide x 10' deep
  - 12' wide x 10' deep
  - 14' wide x 10' deep
- Wood floor on 4 x 6 runners
- Height floor to peak: 10'-11"
- Rear wall height: 7'-3"
- 5'-0" x 6'-9" double-door
- Clerestory windows for added light
- Complete list of materials
- Step-by-step instructions

Price Code P5

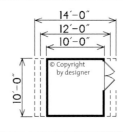

Design #602-002D-4514

STORAGE SHED WITH PLAYHOUSE LOFT

- Size: 12' wide x 12' deep with 2'-8" deep balcony
- Wood floor on concrete piers or concrete floor
- Height floor to peak: 14'-1"
- Ceiling height: 7'-4"
- 4'-0" x 6'-10" single door
- Loft above can be used as playhouse for children
- Loft features ladder for access
- Complete list of materials
- Step-by-step instructions

Price Code P5

Design #602-002D-4518

DELUXE CABANA

- Size: 11'-0" wide x 13'-6" deep
- Concrete floor
- Height floor to peak: 11'-7"
- Ceiling height: 8'-0"
- Unique roof design with skylight
- Convenient dressing room and servicing area
- Perfect storage for poolside furniture and equipment
- Complete list of materials
- Step-by-step instructions

Price Code P6

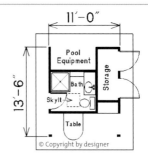

Design #602-002D-4505

CHILDREN'S PLAYHOUSE

- Size: 8' wide x 8' deep
- Wood floor on 4 x 4 runners
- Height floor to peak: 9'-2"
- Ceiling height: 6'-1"
- 2'-deep porch
- Attractive window boxes
- Includes operable windows
- Complete list of materials
- Step-by-step instructions

Price Code P4

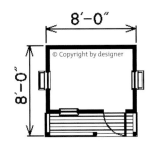

Design #602-002D-4506

CONVENIENCE SHED

- Size: 16' wide x 12' deep
- Concrete floor
- Height floor to peak: 12'-4$\frac{1}{2}$"
- Ceiling height: 8'-0"
- 8'-0" x 7'-0" overhead door
- Ideal for lawn equipment or small boat storage
- Oversized windows brighten interior
- Complete list of materials
- Step-by-step instructions

Price Code P6

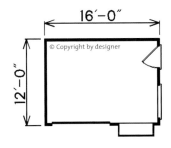

Design #602-002D-4513

GREENHOUSE

- Size: 8' wide x 12' deep
- Gravel floor with concrete foundation wall
- Height foundation to peak: 8'-3"
- An attractive addition to any yard
- Store lawn and garden tools right at hand
- Complete list of materials
- Step-by-step instructions

Price Code P5

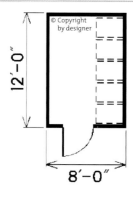

Design #602-002D-4522

GABLE STORAGE SHED/PLAYHOUSE

- Size: 12' wide x 8' deep
- Wood floor on 4 x 4 runners
- Height floor to peak: 10'-5"
- Ceiling height: 8'-0"
- 3'-0" x 6'-8" dutch door
- Perfect for storage or playhouse for children
- Shutters and window box create charming facade
- Complete list of materials
- Step-by-step instructions

Price Code P5

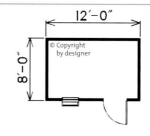

Design #602-002D-4503

GABLE STORAGE SHEDS

- Sizes: 8' wide x 8' deep
           8' wide x 10' deep
           8' wide x 12' deep
           8' wide x 16' deep
- Wood floor on 4 x 4 runners
- Height floor to peak: 8'-4 1/2"
- Ceiling height: 7'-0"
- 4'-0" x 6'-5" double-door
- Complete list of materials
- Step-by-step instructions

Price Code P5

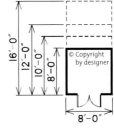

Design #602-002D-4520

YARD BARN WITH LOFT STORAGE

- Size: 10' wide x 12' deep
- Wood floor on 4 x 4 runners
- Height floor to peak: 10'-7"
- Ceiling height: 6'-11"
- 6'-0" x 6'-2" double-door
- Loft provides additional storage area
- Attractive styling is suitable for any yard
- Complete list of materials
- Step-by-step instructions

Price Code P5

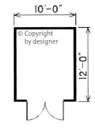

Design #602-002D-4504

GABLE STORAGE SHEDS

- Sizes: 10' wide x 12' deep
  - 10' wide x 16' deep
  - 10' wide x 20' deep
- Wood floor on 4 x 4 runners
- Height floor to peak: 8'-8 $^1/_2$"
- Ceiling height: 7'-0"
- 4'-0" x 6'-4" double-door
- Complete list of materials
- Step-by-step instructions

Price Code P5

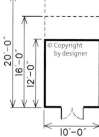

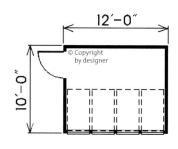

Design #602-002D-4507

GARDEN SHED

- Size: 12' wide x 10' deep
- Wood floor on gravel base
- Height floor to peak: 9'-9"
- Rear wall height: 7'-1$^1/_2$"
- Features skylight windows for optimal plant growth
- Ample room for tool and lawn equipment storage
- Complete list of materials
- Step-by-step instructions

Price Code P5

Design #602-002D-4508

BARN
STORAGE SHEDS

- Sizes: 12' wide x 8' deep
          12' wide x 12' deep
          12' wide x 16' deep
- Wood floor on concrete pier foundation or concrete floor
- Height floor to peak: 9'-10"
- Ceiling height: 7'-10"
- 5'-6" x 6'-8" double-door
- Gambrel roof design
- Complete list of materials
- Step-by-step instructions

Price Code P5

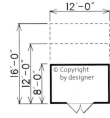

Design #602-002D-4509

GABLE
STORAGE SHEDS

- Sizes: 8' wide x 8' deep
          8' wide x 10' deep
          8' wide x 12' deep
- Wood floor on concrete footings
- Height floor to peak: 9'-1"
- Wall height: 6'-7"
- Circle-top window adds interest and light
- Complete list of materials
- Step-by-step instructions

Price Code P5

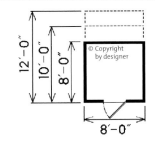

Design #602-002D-4510

MINI-BARN STORAGE SHEDS

- Sizes: 7'-3" wide x 6' deep
  - 7'-3" wide x 8' deep
  - 7'-3" wide x 10' deep
  - 7'-3" wide x 12' deep
- Wood floor on 4 x 6 runners or concrete floor
- Height floor to peak: 9'-0"
- Ceiling height: 7'-4"
- 3'-0" x 6'-8" single door
- Complete list of materials
- Step-by-step instructions

Price Code P5

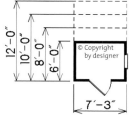

Design #602-002D-4523

GARDEN SHED

- Size: 10' wide x 10' deep
- Wood floor on 4 x 4 runners
- Height floor to peak: 11'-3 $\frac{1}{2}$"
- Left wall height: 8'-0"
- Wonderful complement to any backyard
- Perfect space for lawn equipment or plants and flowers
- Plenty of windows for gardening year-round
- Complete list of materials
- Step-by-step instructions

Price Code P5

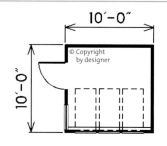

Design #602-002D-4517

CHILDREN'S PLAYHOUSE

- Size: 6' wide x 6' deep
- Wood floor on gravel base
- Height floor to peak: 7'-2"
- Wall height: 4'-4"
- Plenty of windows brighten interior
- Attractive Victorian style
- Gabled doorway and window box add interest
- Complete list of materials
- Step-by-step instructions

Price Code P4

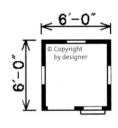

Design #602-002D-4519

SALT BOX STORAGE SHED

- Size: 10' wide x 8' deep
- Wood floor on 4 x 4 runners
- Height floor to peak: 9'-6"
- Front wall height: 8'-0"
- 4'-0" x 6'-8" double-door
- Window adds light to space
- Complete list of materials
- Step-by-step instructions

Price Code P5

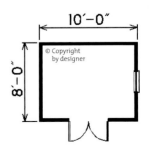

Design #602-002D-4521

BARN STORAGE SHED WITH OVERHEAD LOFT

- Size: 12' wide x 16' deep
- Concrete floor
- Height floor to peak: 12'-5"
- Ceiling height: 8'-0"
- 8' x 7' overhead door for easy entry with large equipment
- Side windows add light
- Complete list of materials
- Step-by-step instructions

Price Code P5

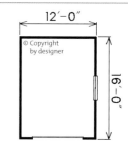

Design #602-002D-4524

MINI BARNS

- Sizes: 8' wide x 8' deep

  8' wide x 10' deep

  8' wide x 12' deep

  8' wide x 16' deep
- Wood floor on 4 x 4 runners
- Height floor to peak: 7'-6"
- Ceiling height: 6'-0"
- 4'-0" x 6'-0" double-door
- Lawn and garden storage
- Complete list of materials
- Step-by-step instructions

Price Code P5

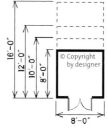

Design #602-002D-6002

2-CAR GARAGE WITH WORKSHOP AND PARTIAL LOFT

- Size: 32' wide x 24' deep
- Building height: 20'-2"
- Roof pitch: 10/12
- Ceiling height: 9'-8"
- Workshop and loft ceiling height: 8'-0"
- 16' x 7' overhead door, 6'-0" x 6'-8" double-door
- Convenient loft above workshop
- Complete list of materials
- Step-by-step instructions

Price Code P8

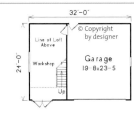

Design #602-002D-6011

3-CAR GARAGE

- Size: 32' wide x 22' deep
- Building height: 12'-2"
- Roof pitch: 4/12
- Ceiling height: 8'-0"
- 9' x 7', 16' x 7' overhead doors
- Side entry for easy access
- Perfect style complements many types of homes
- Complete list of materials
- Step-by-step instructions

Price Code P7

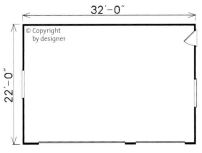

Design #602-002D-6024

2 1/2-CAR GARAGE WESTERN STYLE

- Size: 30' wide x 24' deep
- Building height: 12'-6"
- Roof pitch: 4/12
- Ceiling height: 8'-0"
- Two 9' x 7' overhead doors
- Plenty of storage space
- Additional space is perfect for workshop
- Complete list of materials
- Step-by-step instructions

Price Code P7

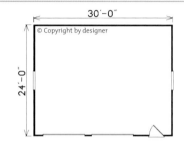

Design #602-002D-6004

2-CAR GARAGE WITH WORKSHOP AND LOFT

- Size: 32' wide x 24' deep
- Building height: 21'-0"
- Roof pitch: 12/12
- Ceiling height: 8'-0"
- Loft ceiling height: 7'-6"
- Two 9' x 7' overhead doors
- Plenty of storage space
- Complete list of materials
- Step-by-step instructions

Price Code P8

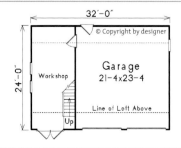

Design #602-002D-6000

2-CAR GARAGE WITH LOFT - GAMBREL ROOF

- Size: 22' wide x 26' deep
- Building height: 20'-7"
- Roof pitch: 7/12, 12/7
- Ceiling height: 8'-0"
- Loft ceiling height: 7'-4"
- Two 9' x 7' overhead doors
- Complete list of materials
- Step-by-step instructions

Price Code P8

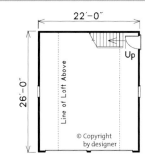

Design #602-002D-6005

1-CAR GARAGE

- Size: 14' wide x 22' deep
- Building height: 10'-10"
- Roof pitch: 4/12
- Ceiling height: 8'-0"
- 9' x 7' overhead door
- Side window enhances exterior
- Convenient side entry
- Complete list of materials
- Step-by-step instructions

Price Code P6

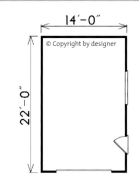

Design #602-002D-6001

2-CAR GARAGE WITH LOFT

- Size: 28' wide x 24' deep
- Building height: 21'-0"
- Roof pitch: 12/12
- Ceiling height: 8'-0"
- Loft ceiling height: 7'-6"
- Two 9' x 7' overhead doors
- Dormers add light and curb appeal
- Complete list of materials
- Step-by-step instructions

Price Code P8

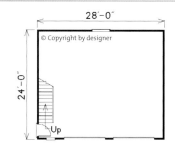

Design #602-002D-6008

2-CAR GARAGE WITH STORAGE-REVERSE GABLE

- Size: 24' wide x 24' deep
- Building height: 12'-8"
- Roof pitch: 4/12
- Ceiling height: 8'-0"
- 16' x 7' overhead door
- Windows on two sides
- Extra space is perfect for storage
- Complete list of materials
- Step-by-step instructions

Price Code P7

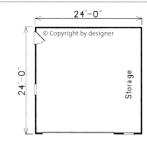

Design #602-002D-6013

2-CAR GARAGE

- Size: 22' wide x 22' deep
- Building height: 12'-2"
- Roof pitch: 4/12
- Ceiling height: 8'-0"
- 16' x 7' overhead door
- Useful side entry
- Perfect for tractor or lawn equipment
- Complete list of materials
- Step-by-step instructions

Price Code P6

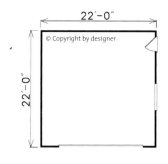

Design #602-002D-6019

2-CAR GARAGE WITH 8' HIGH DOOR

- Size: 24' wide x 26' deep
- Building height: 13'-8"
- Roof pitch: 4/12
- Ceiling height: 9'-0"
- 16' x 8' overhead door
- Practical and appealing
- Side window adds interior light
- Complete list of materials
- Step-by-step instructions

Price Code P7

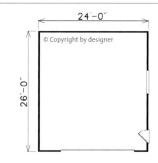

Design #602-002D-6007

2 1/2-CAR GARAGE

- Size: 30' wide x 22' deep
- Building height: 12'-2"
- Roof pitch: 4/12
- Ceiling height: 8'-0"
- 16' x 7' overhead door
- Additional space is perfect for yard equipment storage
- Door allows easy access to and from storage space
- Complete list of materials
- Step-by-step instructions

Price Code P7

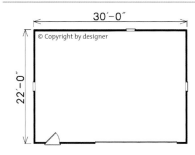

Design #602-002D-6010

1-CAR GARAGE WITH COVERED PORCH

- Size: 24' wide x 22' deep
- Building height: 13'-0"
- Roof pitch: 5/12
- Ceiling height: 8'-0"
- 9' x 7' overhead door
- Distinctive covered porch provides area for entertaining
- Complete list of materials
- Step-by-step instructions

Price Code P7

Design #602–002D–6022

1-CAR GARAGE-WESTERN STYLE

- Size: 14' wide x 22' deep
- Building height: 10'-10"
- Roof pitch: 4/12
- Ceiling height: 8'-0"
- 9' x 7' overhead door
- Compact size is perfect for smaller lots
- Convenient side door
- Complete list of materials
- Step-by-step instructions

Price Code P6

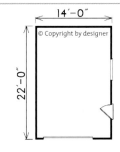

Design #602–002D–6030

2-CAR GARAGE-ATTACHED OR DETACHED

- Size: 22' wide x 24' deep
- Building height: 12'-8"
- Roof pitch: 4/12
- Ceiling height: 8'-0"
- 16' x 7' overhead door
- Convenient front service door
- Traditionally styled
- Complete list of materials
- Step-by-step instructions

Price Code P6

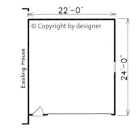

Design #602-002D-6015

2-CAR GARAGE WITH LOFT

- Size: 26' wide x 24' deep
- Building height: 20'-0"
- Roof pitch: 6/12
- Ceiling height: 8'-0"
- Two 9' x 7' overhead doors
- Loft provides extra storage area or workshop space
- Clerestory windows brighten inside
- Complete list of materials
- Step-by-step instructions

Price Code P8

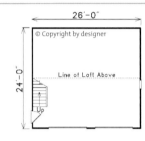

Design #602-002D-6018

2-CAR GARAGE- VICTORIAN

- Size: 24' wide x 24' deep
- Building height: 16'-7"
- Roof pitch: 8/12
- Ceiling height: 8'-0"
- Two 9' x 7' overhead doors
- Accented with Victorian details
- Functional side entry
- Complete list of materials
- Step-by-step instructions

Price Code P7

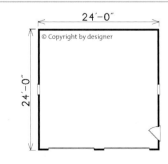

Design #602-002D-6020

3-CAR GARAGE WITH WORKSHOP

- Size: 32' wide x 28' deep
- Building height: 13'-3"
- Roof pitch: 4/12
- Ceiling height: 8'-0"
- 9' x 7', 16' x 7' overhead doors
- Handy workshop space for hobbies
- Convenient side entry door
- Complete list of materials
- Step-by-step instructions

Price Code P7

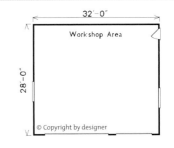

Design #602-002D-6027

2-CAR GARAGE-WESTERN STYLE/ REVERSE GABLE

- Size: 24' wide x 24' deep
- Building height: 16'-7"
- Roof pitch: 8/12
- Ceiling height: 8'-0"
- Two 9' x 7' overhead doors
- Easy, functional design
- Complete list of materials
- Step-by-step instructions

Price Code P7

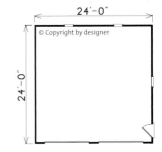

Design #602-002D-6026

3-CAR GARAGE WITH LOFT-WESTERN STYLE

- Size: 32' wide x 24' deep
- Building height: 20'-6"
- Roof pitch: 12/12
- Ceiling height: 8'-0"
- 9' x 7', 16' x 7' overhead doors
- Large side windows draw in light
- Complete list of materials
- Step-by-step instructions

Price Code P8

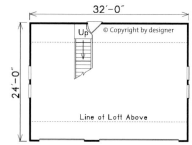

Design #602-002D-6025

3-CAR GARAGE

- Size: 30' wide x 24' deep
- Building height: 13'-8"
- Roof pitch: 5/12
- Ceiling height: 8'-0"
- 9' x 7', 16' x 7' overhead doors
- Highly functional design
- Convenient side entry
- Complete list of materials
- Step-by-step instructions

Price Code P7

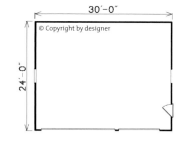

Design #602-002D-6039

2-CAR GARAGE WITH LOFT

- Size: 28' wide x 24' deep
- Building height: 21'-0"
- Roof pitch: 12/12
- Ceiling height: 8'-0"
- Loft ceiling height: 7'-6"
- Two 9' x 7' overhead doors
- Convenient front access door
- Charming dormers add character
- Complete list of materials

Price Code P8

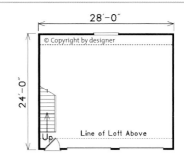

Design #602-002D-6032

2-CAR ECONOMY GARAGE

- Size: 20' wide x 20' deep
- Building height: 11'-10"
- Roof pitch: 4/12
- Ceiling height: 8'-0"
- 16' x 7' overhead door
- Convenient side door
- Complete list of materials
- Step-by-step instructions

Price Code P6

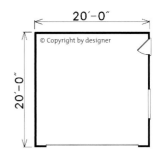

Design #602-002D-6031

2-CAR GARAGE-
GAMBREL ROOF

- Size: 24' wide x 24' deep
- Building height: 15'-5"
- Roof pitch: 4/12, 12/8
- Ceiling height: 8'-0"
- 16' x 7' overhead door
- Attractive addition to any home
- Complete list of materials
- Step-by-step instructions

Price Code P7

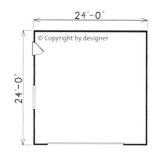

Design #602-002D-6046

3-CAR GARAGE

- Size: 40' wide x 24' deep
- Building height: 15'-6"
- Roof pitch: 6/12
- Ceiling height: 9'-0"
- Three 9' x 7' overhead doors
- Oversized with plenty of room for storage
- Side door for easy access
- Complete list of materials
- Step-by-step instructions

Price Code P7

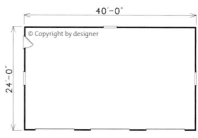

Design #602-002D-6042

3-CAR GARAGE/ WORKSHOP

- Size: 24' wide x 36' deep
- Building height: 14'-6"
- Roof pitch: 4/12
- Ceiling height: 10'-0"
- Three 9' x 8' overhead doors
- Oversized for storage
- Ideal for workshop or maintenance building
- Complete list of materials
- Step-by-step instructions

Price Code P7

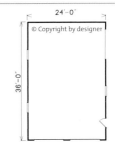

Design #602-002D-6043

1-CAR GARAGE WITH LOFT- GAMBREL ROOF

- Size: 16' wide x 24' deep
- Building height: 18'-9"
- Roof pitch: 6/12, 12/6
- Ceiling height: 8'-0"
- Loft ceiling height: 6'-7"
- 9' x 7' overhead door
- Ideal loft perfect for workshop or storage area
- Complete list of materials
- Step-by-step instructions

Price Code P8

Design #602-002D-6045

2-CAR CARPORT WITH STORAGE

- Size: 24' wide x 24' deep
- Building height: 12'-8"
- Roof pitch: 4/12
- Ceiling height: 8'-0"
- Unique design allows for cars to enter from the front or the side of carport
- Deep storage space for long or tall items
- Complete list of materials
- Step-by-step instructions

Price Code P6

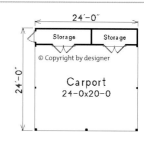

Design #602-002D-7503

POLE BUILDINGS 4 POPULAR SIZES

- Sizes: 24' wide x 32' deep
          24' wide x 40' deep
- Building height: 15'-6"
- Ceiling height: 10'-0"
- Two 5' x 10' sliding doors

- Sizes: 32' wide x 40' deep
          32' wide x 48' deep
- Building height: 17'-6"
- Ceiling height: 12'-0"
- Two 6' x 12' sliding doors

All sizes include:

- Complete list of materials
- Step-by-step instructions

Price Code P8

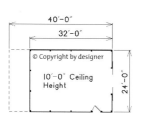

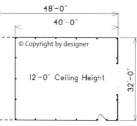

Design #602-002D-6044

3-CAR GARAGE WITH LOFT

- Size: 36' wide x 24' deep
- Building height: 20'-8"
- Roof pitch: 12/12
- Ceiling height: 8'-0"
- Loft ceiling height: 7'-6"
- Three 9' x 7' overhead doors
- Third stall in garage is perfect for boat storage
- Generous loft space for storage or studio
- Complete list of materials
- Step-by-step instructions

Price Code P8

Design #602-002D-7511

POLE BUILDING-HORSE BARN WITH LOFT

- Size: 26' wide x 48' deep
- Building height: 22'-0"
- Roof pitch: 6/12, 12/6
- Loft ceiling height: 11'-0"
- Two 8' x 8' sliding doors
- One 5' x 7' sliding door at loft
- Features four box stalls
- Loft designed for 75 p.s.f. live load
- Complete list of materials
- Step-by-step instructions

Price Code P8

Design #602-002D-7501

MULTI-PURPOSE BARN

- Size: 24' wide x 36' deep
- Building height: 23'-8"
- Roof pitch: 4/12, 12/4
- Loft ceiling height: 9'-9"
- Two 9' x 9' sliding doors
- 5' x 6' loft double-door
- Ideal machine storage or as a three-stall horse barn
- Loft designed for 100 p.s.f. live load
- Complete list of materials
- Step-by-step instructions

Price Code P8

Design #602-002D-7515

POLE BUILDING-OPEN SHED

- Size: 36' wide x 13' deep
- 8' or 10' front wall height
- Lofting storage or machinery storage
- Building can easily be lengthened by adding additional 12' bays
- Complete list of materials
- Step-by-step instructions

Price Code P8

Design #602-002D-7520

WORKROOM WITH COVERED PORCH

- Size: 24' wide x 20' deep
- Building height: 13'-6"
- Roof pitch: 6/12
- Ceiling height: 8'-0"
- Slab foundation
- Easy access through double-doors
- Interior enhanced by large windows
- Large enough for storage
- Complete list of materials
- Step-by-step instructions

Price Code P8

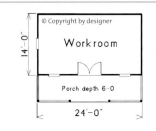

Design #602-002D-7529

3-CAR GARAGE APARTMENT

- 1,040 square feet
- Building height: 23'-0"
- Roof pitch: 5/12
- Ceiling height: 8'-0"
- Three 9' x 7' overhead doors
- 2 bedrooms, 1 bath
- Plan offers second floor laundry, ample cabinets and sliding doors to the deck
- Complete list of materials

Price Code P12

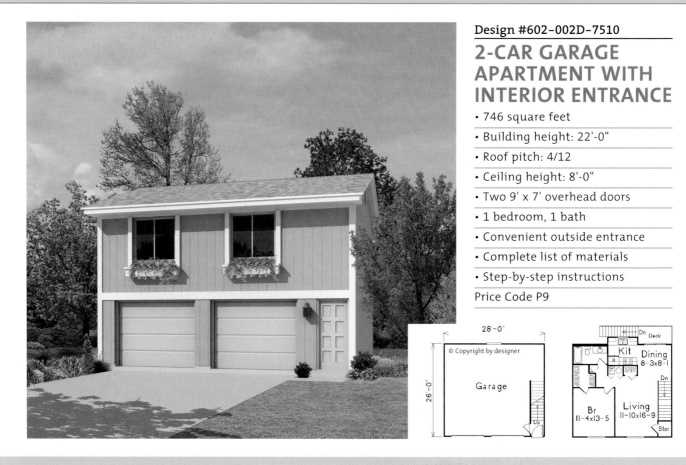

Design #602–002D–7510

2-CAR GARAGE APARTMENT WITH INTERIOR ENTRANCE

- 746 square feet
- Building height: 22'-0"
- Roof pitch: 4/12
- Ceiling height: 8'-0"
- Two 9' x 7' overhead doors
- 1 bedroom, 1 bath
- Convenient outside entrance
- Complete list of materials
- Step-by-step instructions

Price Code P9

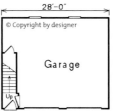

28'-0"
© Copyright by designer
Garage
26'-0"
Up

Dn Deck
Kit
Dining 8–3x8–1
Dn
Br 11–4x13–5
Living 11–10x16–9
Stor

Design #602–002D–7526

2-CAR GARAGE APARTMENT- CAPE COD

- 566 square feet
- Building height: 22'-0"
- Roof pitch: 4.5/12, 12/12
- Ceiling heights: 1st floor 8'-0"
  2nd floor 7'-7"
- Two 9' x 7' overhead doors
- Charming dormers add appeal
- Complete list of materials
- Step-by-step instructions

Price Code P10

28'-0"
© Copyright by designer
Garage
24'-0"
Up

Dn
Studio 18–2x18–4

Design #602–002D–7530

3-CAR GARAGE APARTMENT- CAPE COD

- 813 square feet
- Building height: 22'-0"
- Roof pitch: 4.25/12, 12/12
- Ceiling height: 8'-0"
- Three 9' x 7' overhead doors
- Studio, 1 bath
- Perfect for recreation, in-law suite or home office
- L-shaped kitchen with serving bar
- Complete list of materials

Price Code P12

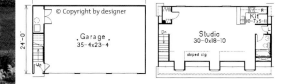

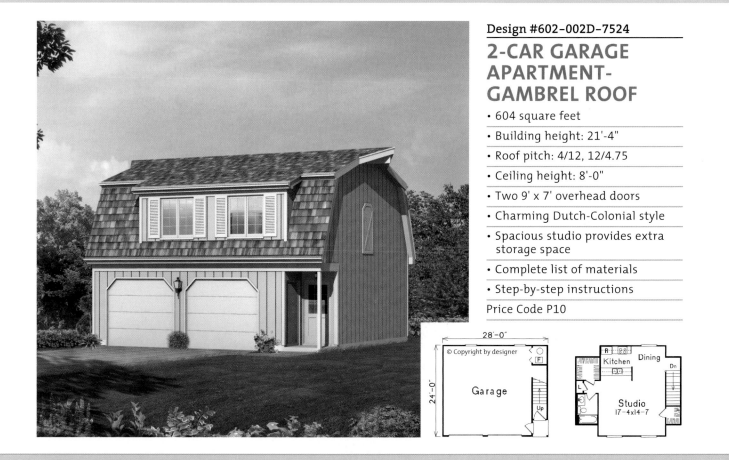

Design #602–002D–7524

2-CAR GARAGE APARTMENT- GAMBREL ROOF

- 604 square feet
- Building height: 21'-4"
- Roof pitch: 4/12, 12/4.75
- Ceiling height: 8'-0"
- Two 9' x 7' overhead doors
- Charming Dutch-Colonial style
- Spacious studio provides extra storage space
- Complete list of materials
- Step-by-step instructions

Price Code P10

INDEX

Credits

ACKNOWLEDGMENTS

Numerous people contributed to this book. In particular, Rick Peters deserves a big thank you for his work on the previous edition. Special thanks to Southern Lumber Co, San Jose, CA.

DESIGNERS

L = Left; R = Right; T = Top; M = Middle; B = Bottom
1: Lane Williams, builder; **2T, 12B, 145:** Robert Giomi & Michael Katz; **5, 31B:** Max Vogt; **6BL, 11T:** Walpole Woodworkers; **6BR, 17T:** Charles Myer/Charles R. Myer & Co., architect; Michael Pollen, builder; **9B, 20:** Tuff Shed; **10:** Harrison Architects; The Northwest EcoBuilding Guild Green Roof Project, roof; Jon Alexander/Sunshine Construction, construction; **11B:** Ana Williamson, architect; **18:** Tom Pellet; **19:** Courtesy Ebeneezer Alden House, Union, Maine; **22:** Riddle Garden Design; **23T, 127T:** Michael Bond; **23B:** Robert Emmett; **25T:** Liz Deck; **28T:** Gary Tintle/Tintle, Inc.; **28B:** Barnpros; **29:** Modern-Shed; **30:** Floribunda Landworks; **32L:** Jeff Mendoza; **32R:** A Gardener's Dream, Nan & Steve Reid, greenhouse design; Nancy McFadden, garden design; **33:** John Holt, woodwork

PHOTOGRAPHERS

Unless otherwise credited, photographs are by **Jamie Hadley**.
Scott Atkinson: 38ML, 38BR, 41 both, 42TL, 42BR, 43TR, 43ML, 46B, 54 all; **Todd Caverly:** 6BM, 12T, 19; **Robin B. Cushman:** 25T, 32R; **Scott Fitzgerrell:** 93R3, 93BR; **Roger Foley:** 22, 30; **Frank Gaglione:** 35M, 39BL; **John Granen:** 7BL, 16 both, 97BR, 134; **Art Gray:** 14; **Rob Harrison:** 10; **Saxon Holt:** 27; **Chuck Kuhn:** 110 both; **Janet Loughrey:** 125T; **Sylvia Martin:** 96BR, 131TR; **E. Andrew McKinney:** 9T; **Olson Photographic/Corner House Stock Photo:** 151T; **Jerry Pavia:** 7BR, 31T; **John Peden:** 6BR, 17T; **Robert Perron:** 58; **Norman A. Plate:** 44, 47TL1, 47TM1, 47TR1, 47TR2, 47MR, 47B; **Melanie Powell/Studio in the Woods:** 111; **Eric Roth:** 3B, 6–7 (main), 8, 13B, 26L; **Susan A. Roth:** 18, 32L, 33; **Mark Rutherford:** 40BR1, 40BR2, 42ML, 42BM, 43TL; **Bonnie Schiffman:** 29; **Thomas J. Story:** 102TR, 103T; **Dan Stultz:** 3T, 137TR, 139T; **Christopher Vendetta:** 2B, 17B, 49TL, 49BR, 56–57 (main), 56BM, 57BL, 57BM, 57BR, 65–67 all, 71TR, 71MR, 72–73 all, 76–79 all, 81T, 82B, 83T, 85–87 all, 90 both, 91TR, 91R2, 91ML, 91BL, 92 both, 93TR, 93R2, 96–97 (main), 96BL, 96BM, 97BL, 97BM, 98, 104, 109T, 112, 118, 122, 128, 140, 146, 153T; **Courtesy of Walpole Woodworkers:** 6BL, 11T; **Peter O. Whiteley:** 125B; **Windquest Companies Inc.:** 35T